Newark-on-Trent: A Sometimes Witty Journey Through Time

Published By Dave Fargher
2025

Index

About the Author – Page 6
A camera-wielding, pun-loving local with a passion for Newark's past.

Preface – Page 8

Introduction – Page 10
The Epic Saga of a Town That Just Wouldn't Quit (and occasionally got bombed, besieged, or bypassed).

Prehistoric to Roman Newark

Chapter 1 – Page 12
The Original Flintstones – Newark's Prehistoric Party Pad
(c. 14,000 BC – c. 4,000 BC)

Chapter 2 – Page 18
From Micro-Flint to Macro-Farms and Henge Goals – The Neolithic & Bronze Age Blockbusters
(c. 4,000 BC – c. 700 BC)

Chapter 3 – Page 28
Torcs, Tribes & Toolkits – Newark's Iron Age Identity
(c. 800 BC – c. 43 AD)

Chapter 4 – Page 34
Pottery, Please – Roman Newark and Its Industrial Might
(43 AD – 410 AD)

Saxons, Vikings & Medieval Mayhem

Chapter 5 – Page 39
From Burhs to Bjarn's Gate – Saxon Newark and Its Viking Visitors
(410 AD – 1066 AD)

Chapter 6 – Page 45
Castles, Kings, and Market Things – Newark's Medieval Majesty
(1066 AD – 1485 AD)

Tudors to Trains

Chapter 7 – Page 50
Wool, Wealth, and Winking at the Crown – Tudor Newark's Textile Triumph
(1485 AD – 1603 AD)

Chapter 8 – Page 57
Sieges, Surrender, and Stuart Shenanigans – Newark in the English Civil War
(1603 AD – 1714 AD)

Chapter 9 – Page 64
The Georgian Era – Canals, Coaches, and a New Dawn
(1714 AD – 1837 AD)

Steam, Sugar & Social Change

Chapter 10 – Page 70
Steam, Sugar, and Social Strife – Newark in the Victorian Era
(1837 AD – 1901 AD)

Chapter 11 – Page 76
Wars, Waves, and a Changing World – Newark in the 20th Century
(1901 AD – 2000 AD)

Digital Age & Local Legends

Chapter 12 – Page 82
Revival, and the Digital Age – Newark in the 21st Century
(2000 AD – Present Day)

Additional

Outro – Page 87
Still Standing, Still Selling, Still Slightly Sarcastic

Timeline – Page 90
Newark-on-Trent: A Brief History with Extra Sass

The Historic Buildings of Newark – Page 94

Former Factories – Page 100

Historic Points of Interest – Page 111

Notable Historic Sites – Page 121

Ad Pontem – Page 122
Newark's Roman Service Station

Crococalana – Page 124
The Roman Town That Time (Almost) Forgot

Margidunum – Page 126
The Roman Roundabout Before Newark

Queen Sconce – Page 128

Battle of Stoke Field – Page 130

The Newark Torc
Newark's Golden Halo of Mystery– Page 133

Twelve Sides of Confusion
The Norton Disney Dodecahedron– Page 136

The Myth of The Newark Tunnels – 138

The Walls and Gates of Newark - 141

More Books – 144

A special creative treat – Page 147

Free Guide to Newark On Trent

About the Author

Dave Fargher is Newark-on-Trent's unofficial heritage whisperer. Born and raised in the town, Dave has made it his mission to ensure Newark's history isn't just remembered — it's celebrated, shared, and occasionally laughed at.

In 2021, he founded the *Newark on Trent Photographs* Facebook group, which quickly grew into a fantastic online community with thousands. What started as a place to post scenic snaps and nostalgic street scenes has become a digital town square — part photo archive, part memory lane, and part "spot the Bank that used to be a Pub that used to be a Bank but is now a pub….or Bank."

But Dave didn't stop there. In 2025, he launched www.newarkguide.co.uk, a free, interactive digital gateway to Newark's past and present. The site includes historic buildings, curiosities, parks, pubs, former breweries, and even the occasional ghost story. It's part history lesson, part treasure hunt, and entirely brilliant

The Newark Guide isn't just a website — it's a love letter to the town. It includes local legends, industrial heritage, walking routes, event listings, and a growing archive of photos and videos. It's been praised by residents, businesses, and tourists alike, and has helped put Newark's quirks and charms firmly on the digital map.

Dave also gives talks, supports local heritage groups, and has been a guest speaker at community events.

Whether he's photographing forgotten corners, unearthing medieval trivia, or explaining why "gate" means "street" (thanks, Vikings), Dave is always championing Newark's story — with wit, warmth, and a healthy dose of historical sass.

When he's not writing, mapping, or myth-busting, you'll find him wandering the town with a camera in one hand and a factoid in the other, ready to tell anyone who'll listen why Newark is the most fascinating place you've never quite appreciated properly. Until now.

Dave's mission? To make history accessible, hilarious, and just a little bit sassy. Whether he's mapping, snapping, or writing, he's always championing Newark's past with a wink, a grin, and a well-timed pun.

Preface

The information in this book has been lovingly cobbled together from a wide range of sources, including archaeological reports, historical records, local archives, museum exhibits, and the occasional dog walk conversation. Every effort has been made to ensure accuracy, and the facts presented are true to the best of the author's knowledge.

That said, this is not a peer-reviewed academic tome. It's a local history book written by a proud amateur with a passion for Newark-on-Trent, a camera in one hand, and a sarcasm dial permanently stuck on "mildly cheeky." The humour throughout is intentional and used to make history more engaging, not to diminish its importance or the people involved.

If you spot a factual error, a typo, or a joke that made you groan audibly — congratulations, you're now part of the historical process. Corrections, suggestions, and compliments (especially the last one) are always welcome.

Now, back to the flint tools, cannonballs, and questionable royal decisions.

Oh, I'm not an artist, so excuse the pictures. They're more a visual aide then a realistic work of art
:)

Thanks to:

Colette, Louis and the rest of the Farghers.

Special Thanks

All the people of Newark, past and present.
Tess Machling (Big Book of Torcs)
David Marshall (History of Brewing in Newark on Trent)
Ian Woods
Kevin Winter
Newark Civil War Museum
Newark Civic Trust

&
Mellina

Oh, and the Internet for providing a wealth of information and a seemingly endless supply of cat videos.

You helped me procrastinate in style

Introduction: The Epic Saga of a Town That Just Wouldn't Quit

Alright, listen up, you magnificent, insatiably curious time-travelling beauties! Ever wondered about Newark-on-Trent? Yeah, that seemingly quaint market town in Nottinghamshire?

Well, buckle up your metaphorical seatbelts, because it turns out this place has more layers than a historical onion, and it's far less inclined to make you cry (unless you stub your toe on an ancient Roman pot, which, admittedly, can be quite painful). But this time, we're peeling back *all* the layers.

We're going for the full archaeological, architectural, and anecdotal deep dive.

There are no dry dates, no droning footnotes, and absolutely no apologies for the puns. Instead, you're about to embark on a time-travelling tour through the town's entire history.

This isn't just some dusty old chronicle; this is a wild, often hilarious, journey through millennia. We're talking 14,000 years of human shenanigans. From the very first "locals" who probably thought flint was the height of technology (bless their hearts), to Roman industrial magnates who clearly skipped "Naming Towns 101," Saxon warlords who just wanted a nice "new work," medieval monarchs with questionable hygiene and very bad bowel movements, and a starring role in the English Civil War that was basically a very long, very messy, family squabble.

But we're also going to explore the nooks and crannies: the lingering echoes of wartime bombings (even if they were a bit *random*), the peculiar tales, the whispered legends of secret tunnels beneath the town, and the often-overlooked history of Newark's very own defensive walls. Because sometimes, the weirdest stories are the best ones.

So, ditch your preconceptions, grab your preferred beverage (something strong, perhaps, to prepare for the sheer absurdity of human history), and prepare to uncover the glorious, messy, and utterly fascinating past of Newark-on-Trent.

We promise details, dates, intriguing characters, and enough snark to keep you thoroughly entertained. After all, history's best served with a smile, a knowing wink, and possibly a well-timed eye-roll at humanity's past decisions

.

Let's dig in - trowel optional, enthusiasm mandatory.

For any places mentioned, you can find more information on
www.newarkguide.co.uk

you can also see locations of places mentioned on the interactive map (with over 250 plotted locations

https://www.newarkguide.co.uk/interactive-map

Chapter 1: The Original Flintstones – Newark's Prehistoric Party Pad

(c. 14,000 BC – c. 4,000 BC)
BYO Mammoth! And Mind the Micro-Scrapers

Welcome to Newark: Before the Romans, Before the Saxons… Before the Concept of Socks

Long before Newark-on-Trent had a castle, a market square, or a Greggs, it had flint. And not just a few pebbles you'd kick on a bad day - no, we're talking industrial quantities of the stuff, practically begging to be chipped, flaked, and turned into something sharp and useful. This was the original B&Q, minus the loyalty card. A place where "home improvement" meant sharpening a stick with another, very specific, pointy rock. And yes, even back then, there were probably domestic disputes:

"Gerald, I told you not to use my best scraper on that mammoth hide!"

"Sorry, Brenda, it was either that or gnaw it off with my teeth again."

England on the Edge: The Late Palaeolithic and Mesolithic Eras

To understand Newark's prehistoric appeal, we must rewind to around 14,000 BC, when Britain was still shaking off the last Ice Age like a hungover mammoth. The glaciers were retreating - grudgingly — and the land was a windswept tundra. Think less "rolling English countryside" and more "Siberian steppe with commitment issues."

This was a world of megafauna: woolly mammoths, wild horses, bison, and the now-extinct giant deer (Megaloceros, for those who like their Latin with a side of extinction). Humans were nomadic hunter-gatherers, following the herds, living in temporary shelters, and crafting tools from stone, bone, and antler. They didn't have coffee, but they did have mammoth steaks and a deep understanding of animal behaviour. And probably a lot of blisters.

By around 10,000 BC, the climate warmed dramatically, ushering in the Mesolithic (Middle Stone Age). The tundra gave way to dense forests of birch, pine, and eventually oak and elm. The megafauna dwindled, replaced by red deer, roe deer, and wild boar. Hunting strategies had to adapt. Out went the big, clunky tools of the Palaeolithic; in came the microliths—tiny, razor-sharp flint flakes mounted on wooden shafts to make arrows, harpoons, and other composite tools. Think of it as the Swiss Army knife of the Stone Age—if the Swiss had been barefoot and covered in elk hide.

Newark's Prehistoric Allure: Location, Location, Location

So why Newark? Why did this particular patch of Nottinghamshire become the prehistoric equivalent of a five-star resort?

Simple: the River Trent.

In the Mesolithic, the Trent wasn't just a river—it was a superhighway. A natural corridor through the landscape, it guided migrating animals and thirsty humans alike. It was the M25 of mammal migration, minus the traffic cones and with slightly more chance of being eaten. Herds of red deer and wild horses would have followed its banks, and our ancestors—let's call them Team Prehistoric—knew a good ambush spot when they saw one.

They set up seasonal camps at what we now call Farndon Fields, just a flint's throw from the river. Elevated ground offered perfect vantage points. The river's bends and shallows made ideal hunting traps. It was a drive-thru for dinner, with fewer queues and considerably more danger.

And it wasn't just Newark. The wider Nottinghamshire area was a prehistoric playground. Sherwood Forest? Once a dense, ancient woodland teeming with game and mystery. Southwell? Probably a nice spot for a riverside barbecue. And Edwinstowe? Well, it wasn't named after a saint yet, but it was likely a decent place to dry your mammoth-hide trousers.

Their shelters were likely made from branches, hides, and whatever else they could scavenge. Think less "glamping" and more "survivalist chic." They foraged for berries, nuts, and roots, and cooked their prey over open fires. And yes, they probably had a sense of humour.

"Brenda, you call that a scraper? My grandmother could make a better blade with her teeth—and she's been a skeleton for a thousand years!"

The Flint Revelation: Unearthing Newark's Ancient Story

Between 1991 and 2018, archaeologists from the Farndon Archaeological Research Institute (FARI) — a group of very patient people with trowels and a high tolerance for mud — got their knees dirty at Farndon Fields. What they found was nothing short of spectacular: a treasure trove of flint tools.

We're talking scrapers for preparing hides, blades for butchering, and projectile points for spears and darts. These weren't just random rocks — they were precision instruments, crafted with skill and care. The sheer variety of styles suggests that this wasn't just one family's toolkit. Newark was a hotspot. A prehistoric Airbnb. A place where different groups, from different regions, returned again and again.

Imagine the cultural exchange:

"Nice microlith, where'd you get it?"

"Traded it with a bloke from the Ouse Valley. He throws in a free boar tusk if you haggle."

The continuity of occupation at Farndon Fields suggests a deep, ancestral knowledge of the land. These people knew where the game would be, where the flint was best, and how to make the most of the landscape. They weren't just surviving — they were thriving, innovating, and leaving behind a legacy that we're still uncovering today.

Conclusion: The First Chapter in Newark's Long Story

So there you have it. Long before Newark had pubs, politics, or parking problems, it had people. People who hunted, crafted, laughed, and lived along the banks of the River Trent. They left behind no written records, no monuments, and no Instagram selfies — but they did leave flint. Lots and lots of flint.

And from that flint, we've pieced together the first chapter in Newark's long, strange, and utterly fascinating story. A story that stretches from mammoth steaks to market stalls, from microliths to Morrisons. And we're just getting started.

**Chapter 2: From Micro-Flint to Macro-Farms and Henge Goals
– The Neolithic & Bronze Age Blockbusters**

(c. 4,000 BC – c. 700 BC)
Now with More Permanent Residences and Ancient Party Circles!

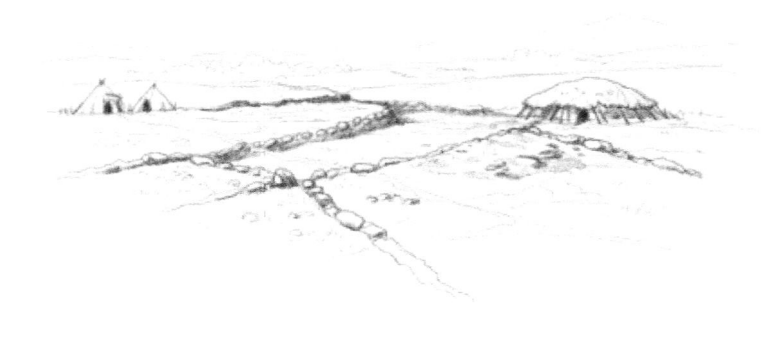

Part 1: The Neolithic – Neighbours, Nettles, and Neolithic Know-How (c. 4,000–2,500 BC)

If Chapter 1 was all about flint, fur, and fast-moving mammoths, Chapter 2 is where things slow down, settle in, and start sprouting. Welcome to the Neolithic — when humans finally decided that chasing dinner across the tundra was exhausting and perhaps it was time to grow it instead. This was the dawn of agriculture, the original "grow-your-own" movement, and Newark and its neighbours were right there in the thick of it.

The River Trent, once a mammoth motorway, now flowed past budding farms and the first whispers of permanent homes. The Mesolithic wanderers had hung up their spears and picked up hoes — though not the kind you'd find at B&Q.

Yet.

Across Nottinghamshire, the story was similar. The Sherwood Forest area — long before it was full of outlaws and interpretive signage — was being cleared for crops. Southwell may have been a sacred site long before it had a Minster, and the future site of Mansfield was probably just a muddy field with excellent drainage and a few confused aurochs.

Tools of the Trade: From Axe to Allotment

The Neolithic toolkit was a polished upgrade — literally. Gone were the rough flint scrapers of old; in came the polished stone axe, the Rambo knife of its day. These weren't just tools — they were status symbols. Some were made from exotic stone sourced from Cumbria's Langdale axe factories, over 150 miles away. That's right: Newarkians were importing designer axes before it was cool.

And it wasn't just tools. Pottery sherds—some plain, others with geometric flair—hint at a more settled, domestic life. You don't lug fragile pots around if you're constantly on the move. These were signs of permanence: homes with hearths, storage pits, and possibly the first proto-kitchens (though no evidence of sourdough starters has yet been found, despite our best hopes).

One particularly delightful find from a Newark excavation? A Neolithic axe reused as a whetstone. That's right—upcycling, 6,000 years before Pinterest. Our ancestors were not only practical, they were sustainable. Greta Thunberg would be proud.

Farming, Feasting, and Flinty Friendships

With farming came community. You can't plough a field or raise livestock without a bit of cooperation (and probably a few arguments about whose goat ate whose barley). These early farmers possibly lived in small, kin-based groups, building longhouses or timber-framed dwellings with thatched roofs and earthen floors. Think "Grand Designs: Prehistoric Edition."

But life wasn't all toil. The Neolithic also saw the rise of ritual and monument building—a sign that people had not only the time but the spiritual curiosity to ponder life's bigger questions.

Across Britain, this era gave birth to causewayed enclosures, long barrows, and the earliest henges—circular earthworks that would evolve into the great ceremonial sites of the Bronze Age.

While Newark doesn't boast a Stonehenge of its own (yet), the surrounding region was certainly part of this ritual landscape. Places like Creswell Crags and the Vale of Belvoir were buzzing with seasonal feasts, ceremonies, and the occasional prehistoric knees-up. Picture it: firelight, drums, roast boar and, someone inevitably overdoing it on the fermented berry juice.

The Middlebeck Henge: Newark's Ancient VIP Lounge

Between 2016 and 2017, archaeologists from Oxford Archaeology North made a discovery that would make any prehistorian's heart skip a beat: a henge monument at Middlebeck, just south of Newark. Dating to around 3,300 BC (late Neolithic/early bronze age), it's one of the earliest known henge monuments in Britain.

This wasn't just a ditch in the ground. The Middlebeck henge was a carefully constructed circular enclosure, likely surrounded by timber posts and accessed via a raised causeway. It was built near a natural spring—because even then, location mattered. Was it a temple? A gathering place? A prehistoric picnic spot? We may never know for sure, but its very existence tells us that the people of Newark were thinking big.

Newark's Neolithic Niche

So why Newark? Why did this patch of Nottinghamshire continue to attract people long after the mammoths had moved on?

Simple: geography. The River Trent remained a vital artery — not just for water and food, but for communication and trade. It connected communities, carried goods, and probably served as a spiritual boundary as well. The fertile floodplains were ideal for early agriculture, and the elevated ground offered protection from floods and a commanding view of the landscape (and your neighbour's suspiciously large turnips).

The archaeological finds from this period — axes, pottery, field systems — suggest that Newark was more than just a farming outpost. It was a hub. A place where people gathered, exchanged goods, and perhaps even ideas. The continuity of occupation from the Mesolithic into the Neolithic speaks to a deep-rooted connection to the land, a recognition of its value that transcended generations. Or maybe they just really liked the view.

Part 2: The Bronze Age – Bling and Burials
(c. 2,500 BC – c. 700 BC)

If the Neolithic was about settling down and learning to farm, the Bronze Age was about levelling up. Around 2,500 BC, someone figured out that if you mix copper with a bit of tin, you get bronze—a shiny, durable, and altogether more impressive material than stone. Cue the prehistoric equivalent of a tech boom. Tools were sharper, weapons deadlier, and jewellery was seriously upgraded.

Burials, Beads, and Bronze Age Bling

The Middlebeck site wasn't just about ceremonies. It was also a cemetery. Archaeologists uncovered 35 cremation burials, many of them accompanied by urns, beads, and other grave goods. These weren't haphazard interments—they were carefully arranged, suggesting a community that honoured its dead with ritual and respect.
Among the finds were delicate necklace beads, likely worn by the deceased in life and carried with them into the afterlife. There was also a beautifully polished stone axe—originally from Langdale in Cumbria—found buried alongside Iron Age pottery. That's a 2,000-year-old heirloom, folks. Either someone had a serious sentimental streak, or they were just really good at not losing things.

Life in Bronze Age Newark: Fields, Forges, and Family Feasts

So what was daily life like in Bronze Age Newark? Picture small farming communities living in roundhouses—circular dwellings with wattle-and-daub walls and thatched roofs. These homes were warm, practical, and surprisingly spacious. Families would have cooked over open hearths, stored grain in pits, and slept on beds of straw and animal skins.

Farming was now the norm. People grew barley and wheat, kept cattle and sheep, and supplemented their diet with wild berries, nuts, and the occasional unlucky deer. Tools were made of bronze—axes, sickles, and knives that were sharper, more durable, and far more stylish than their stone predecessors. And then there were the social gatherings. The Bronze Age saw the rise of communal feasting, often tied to seasonal festivals or funerary rites. Imagine a summer solstice celebration by the henge: fires blazing, meat roasting, drums beating and, someone inevitably trying to dance after too much fermented honey water.

Trade and Travel: Newark's Bronze Age Network

Newark wasn't isolated. The River Trent continued to serve as a vital artery for trade and communication. Goods, ideas, and people flowed between its banks, connecting Newark to other communities across Britain and beyond. The presence of Langdale axes and exotic beads suggests long-distance trade networks, possibly stretching as far as Ireland and continental Europe

Bronze itself was a traded commodity. Tin was rare and had to be imported, often from Cornwall or Brittany. That meant Newark's metalworkers were part of a much larger economic system—one that required negotiation, cooperation, and a fair bit of travel. Think of it as the Bronze Age version of LinkedIn, but with more oxen and fewer endorsements.

Conclusion: From Flint to Foundations

By the end of the Bronze Age, Newark had firmly established itself as a place of significance. It was no longer just a seasonal hunting ground—it was a community, a ceremonial centre, and a hub of trade and innovation. The people who lived here weren't just surviving—they were building a legacy.
They left behind henges, burials, and artefacts that still speak to us across the millennia. They turned flint into finesse, and stone into story. And they laid the foundations—quite literally—for the Iron Age societies that would follow.

Chapter 3: Torcs, Tribes & Toolkits – Newark's Iron Age Identity
(c. 800 BC – c. 43 AD)
Less Iron Man, More Iron Bling… and Pre-Roman Walls!

Iron: The New Bronze (But Sharper)

Welcome to the Iron Age—where the tools stengthened, the jewellery was a lot flashier, and the neighbours were perhaps a bit more territorial. Around 800 BC, humanity collectively decided that bronze—while shiny and respectable—just wasn't cutting it anymore (literally). Enter iron: stronger, more abundant, and perfect for everything from ploughshares to pointy things. It was the prehistoric equivalent of upgrading from a flip phone to a smartphone—suddenly, everything was faster, sharper, and more efficient.

In Newark-on-Trent and the wider Sherwood area, this era marked a new chapter of settled life, tribal identity, and technological innovation. Gone were the days of wandering bands and temporary shelters. Instead, we see the rise of roundhouses, field systems, and fortified settlements. The people of Newark were now part of a broader cultural and political landscape, one defined by tribes, trade, and the occasional turf war over who had the best sheep.

And yes, while Newark was busy digging ditches and forging iron, nearby South Muskham was also getting in on the action. Excavations there revealed a full-blown Iron Age settlement, complete with enclosures and domestic structures. Clearly, the Newark area was more than just a pretty riverside—it was a prehistoric hotspot.

Meet the Corieltauvi: Newark's Iron Age Tribe

Newark sat comfortably within the lands of the Corieltauvi, a tribe known more for their agricultural prowess than their appetite for conquest. Their capital was Ratae

Corieltauvorum — modern-day Leicester — and they were the kind of tribe that probably brought homemade mead to every gathering and knew how to rotate their crops. Peaceful, practical, and proud, the Corieltauvi were the Iron Age equivalent of the reliable neighbours who always return your tools and never let their pigs wander into your barley.

But they weren't alone. The Iron Age was a patchwork of tribal territories, each with its own customs, leaders, and boundaries. To the north were the Brigantes, known for their fierce independence and formidable queens. To the east, the Iceni — yes, the tribe of Boudica fame. To the south, the Catuvellauni, who were a bit more ambitious (read: pushy). It was a time of tribal diplomacy, occasional skirmishes, and a very clear understanding of where your land ended and someone else's began.

"Oi, Gareth, that's our ditch — move your goats!"

Life in Iron Age Newark: Roundhouses, Ditches & Domestic Bliss

Archaeological digs east of Bowbridge Lane have revealed the remains of a substantial Iron Age settlement . We're talking nearly a dozen roundhouses, ditched enclosures, pits, and even a possible square barrow — because nothing says "we've made it" like a geometrically precise burial mound.

These roundhouses were the Iron Age's answer to open-plan living. Circular, thatched, and surprisingly roomy, they were the heart of family life. Meals were cooked over central hearths, stories were shared, and winters were endured with a lot of wool and a little luck. Surrounding these homes were deep ditches — field boundaries, livestock pens, and possibly even defensive perimeters. These weren't castles, but they were practical, multipurpose earthworks that showed a community thinking ahead.

And yes, there was pottery — always pottery. Because what's an archaeological dig without a few good Sherds?

In a delightful twist of continuity, that Neolithic axe-turned-whetstone made another appearance. Still in use, still sharpening blades, and still proving that recycling is timeless. It's a touching reminder that Iron Age Newarkians respected their tools — and their ancestors — enough to keep using them long after the original handle had rotted away.

Iron Age Bling: The Newark Torc

Now, let's talk jewellery. Because while the Iron Age was practical, it also had a flair for the dramatic. Enter the Newark Torc — a stunning gold neck ornament discovered in 2005 by a very lucky metal detectorist (Maurice Richardson). Dated between 250–50 BC, this masterpiece of Celtic craftsmanship features intricate decoration and a level of artistry that would make any modern jeweller weep with envy.

Torcs weren't just accessories; they were symbols of power and prestige, worn by chieftains, Chieftesses, warriors, and possibly the Iron Age equivalent of influencers. The Newark Torc is a statement piece — Iron Age haute couture — and it raises tantalising questions. What ceremonies did it grace? What stories could it tell? Probably something about a particularly dramatic tribal gathering or a legendary hunt gone wrong. Or maybe just a really good party.

Tools of the Trade: Weaving, Warring & Working the Land

The Iron Age toolkit was as diverse as it was practical. At Newark's Civil War Museum (which, despite the name, houses artefacts from far beyond the 17th century), you'll find bone weaving combs, loom weights, and dagger fragments — each one a window into daily life. These items speak of textile production, personal defence, and the everyday grind of making clothes, tools, and meals from scratch.

The presence of such objects suggests a thriving domestic economy, where people weren't just surviving — they were crafting, trading, and expressing themselves through their work. Whether it was weaving a tunic, forging a blade, or decorating a pot, the people of Iron Age Newark were skilled, creative, and deeply connected to their environment.

Newark's Ancient Walls: Before the Castle Came the Ramparts

Before Newark became known for its imposing medieval castle, it had another line of defence: Iron Age ramparts. These weren't stone walls but massive earthen banks, topped with timber palisades and fronted by deep ditches. They encircled the settlement, offering protection and a clear boundary — a prehistoric "keep out" sign for would-be intruders.

These defences were likely repurposed by later settlers, including the Anglo-Saxons, who built their "New Work" (or burh) atop the existing earthworks. It's a testament to the strategic importance of Newark's location and the continuity of settlement that stretches back thousands of years. Long before the Normans arrived with their stone and mortar, Newark's people were already thinking defensively — and building accordingly.

Final Thoughts: Iron Age Newark – A Community Forged in Metal and Memory

The Iron Age was a time of innovation, identity, and ingenuity. Newark's inhabitants weren't just passive dwellers in a changing world — they were active participants, shaping their landscape, crafting their tools, and expressing their culture in gold, clay, and earth. From the humble roundhouse to the dazzling torc, their legacy lives on in the soil beneath our feet and the stories we continue to uncover.

And if you ever find yourself walking through Newark's streets and wondering why the place feels so rooted, so layered, and so oddly fond of ditches — well, now you know. It's been that way for over 2,000 years.

Chapter 4: Pottery, Please – Roman Newark and Its Industrial Might
(43 AD – 410 AD)
We're Just Visiting, Apparently, But We're Making LOTS of Pots

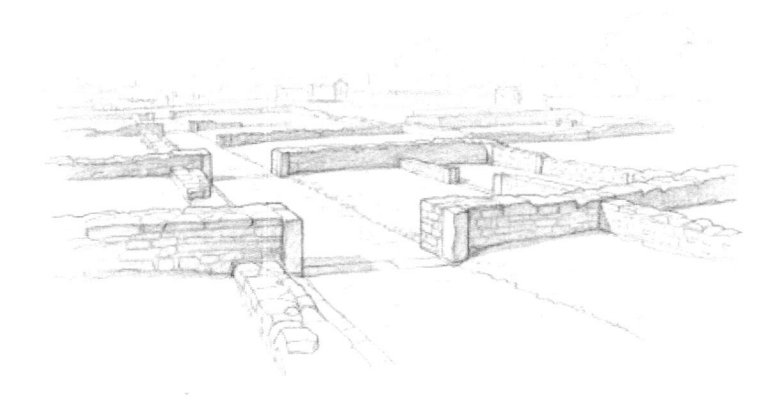

Welcome to Roman Britain: Now With Roads, Baths, and Bureaucracy

Ah, the Romans. Masters of roads, rulers of empires, and absolute sticklers for naming things. From latrines to legionary outposts, they labelled everything with Latin precision. So, you'd think Newark would've earned a spot on the Roman map, right? A nice little name like *Novus Arcus* or *Potteria Maxima*.

But no. While nearby settlements like Margidunum (modern Bingham), Ad Pontem (East Stoke), and Crococolana (Brough) got their moment in the imperial spotlight, Newark was left off the Antonine Itinerary. No fanfare. No Latinised glory. Just... omitted. Like being left off the guest list to the biggest toga party of the century.

But don't be fooled by the cartographic cold shoulder. Newark was very much alive and kicking during the Roman occupation — and not just kicking, but firing up kilns, housing travellers, and churning out pottery like it was going out of fashion (which, to be fair, it never did).

Newark: The Roman Service Station (With Bonus Beer)

Despite the lack of a Roman name, Newark's strategic location made it a natural hub. Nestled between the mighty Fosse Way — that diagonal Roman superhighway slicing across Britain — and the ever-reliable River Trent, Newark was the perfect pit stop. Think of it as the Welcome Break of Roman Britain: a place to rest your sandals, water your horse, and maybe pick up a few amphorae on the way to Lincoln.

And yes, there was beer. The 19th-century construction boom along Northgate—particularly the building of breweries, unearthed a treasure trove of Roman artefacts and structural remains. Clearly, the Romans weren't just passing through; they were living, working, and brewing. After all, what's a Roman road trip without a bit of *cervisia*?

Villas, Mosaics, and Mysterious Dodecahedrons

Zoom out a little, and the wider Newark and Sherwood area reveals a Romanised landscape brimming with activity. Sites at Southwell, Norton Disney, and Car Colston have yielded villas, mosaics, and even hypocaust heating systems—because central heating isn't a modern luxury, it's a Roman legacy. These were the homes of the well-to-do, the Roman equivalent of countryside retreats with underfloor heating and a nice view of the barley fields.

And then there's the Norton Disney dodecahedron—a baffling bronze object with twelve flat faces, each with a hole of varying size. Found over Europe (130 or so, 30 from UK), it's the Rubik's Cube of antiquity. Was it a calendar? A game? A surveying tool? Or just a very fancy way to decide who had to clean the latrines? The mystery remains, but it's a delightful reminder that even the Romans had their quirks.

The Middlebeck Revelation: Newark's Pottery Empire

Now, let's talk about the real blockbuster: the Middlebeck archaeological dig. This wasn't just a few potsherds and a rusty brooch. This was a game-changing discovery. Archaeologists uncovered a staggering 73 Roman pottery kilns

. Yes, seventy-three. That's not a cottage industry—that's a ceramic empire.

These kilns were remarkably well-preserved and showed signs of continuous use over a long period. This wasn't a side hustle; it was a full-blown industrial operation, one of the largest Roman pottery production sites in Britain. Suddenly, Newark wasn't just a convenient stopover—it was a manufacturing powerhouse, supplying pots, tiles, and amphorae to homes, garrisons, and markets across the province.

Imagine the scale: coarseware for everyday use, Samian ware for the fancy folk, amphorae for transporting wine and olive oil, and roof tiles for those stylish Roman villas. All of it fired right here, in the kilns of Middlebeck. It's a testament to Newark's strategic location, natural resources (hello, clay-rich riverbanks), and skilled labour force. This was Roman Newark's moment— not on the map, perhaps, but firmly in the economic engine of Britannia.

No Name, No Problem

So, Newark didn't get a Latin name. Big deal. It was too busy making pots, housing travellers, and fuelling the Roman economy to worry about imperial branding. It may not have been Verulamium, but it was vital—a place of industry, ingenuity, and quiet importance.

And who knows? Maybe the locals liked it that way. No Roman tax collectors sniffing around, no imperial inspectors asking awkward questions about kiln emissions. Just good, honest work—and a lot of it.

Final Thoughts: Newark's Roman Legacy

The Roman era in Newark wasn't about grand forums or marble temples. It was about craftsmanship, commerce, and community. From the kilns of Middlebeck to the villas of Southwell, the story is one of everyday excellence—of people who built, brewed, and baked their way into history.

So next time you pass through Newark, spare a thought for the potters of the past. They may not have had a Latin postcode, but they left behind a legacy that still shapes the landscape—one Sherd at a time.

Chapter 5: From Burhs to Bjarn's Gate – Saxon Newark and Its Viking Visitors
(410 AD – 1066 AD)
The Original "New Work" From Home, Now with More Raids!

Goodbye Romans, Hello Raids

When the Romans finally packed up their sandals and scrolls around 410 AD, they didn't so much exit stage left as vanish into the mist, leaving behind roads, ruins, and a lot of confused locals. Britain, once a well-oiled cog in the imperial machine, was now on its own. Cue the arrival of new players: the Anglo-Saxons, the Vikings, and eventually, the Normans. But before the castles and cathedrals, Newark was already busy reinventing itself.

This period, often unfairly dubbed the "Dark Ages," was anything but dim for Newark and Sherwood. It was a time of fortification, fusion, and fierce identity-building. The town began to forge its own medieval mojo, blending Saxon resilience with Norse flair and a growing Christian conscience. And while the archaeological record in Nottinghamshire is a bit patchy (think "pinpricks of light in a fog of uncertainty"), what we do know paints a picture of a region adapting, evolving, and occasionally being raided by people with excellent beards.

The Birth of the "New Work"

Enter the burh—Old English for "fortified settlement" and the medieval equivalent of a gated community with serious attitude. Newark, perched strategically on the River Trent, was a prime candidate for such a transformation. With its earthen ramparts, timber palisades, and deep defensive ditches, it became a beacon of stability in a turbulent world. Think of it as the Saxon version of a security system, complete with moat and muscle.

And the name? "Newark" its thought it derives from "Neue Werk" — literally "New Work." Less like a medieval startup and more like a bold declaration: "We've built something new, and it's here to stay." But what about the "Old Work"? That's the historical equivalent of a lost prequel. Some whisper of Farndon, others of Southwell, but the truth remains buried — possibly under someone's garden gnome collection. One day, perhaps, a rogue archaeologist will stumble upon it and rewrite Newark's origin story.

Minting, Mourning, and Millgate Mysteries

Newark's growing importance in the Anglo-Saxon period is stamped — quite literally — in metal. A coin from the reign of King Edwy (d. 957 AD) was discovered here, suggesting Newark had its own mint. That's right — Newark was printing its own money while other towns were still bartering with chickens. It's a clear sign of economic clout and royal recognition, long before the Normans came knocking.

Meanwhile, over on Millgate, things were heating up — quite literally. In the 1960s, archaeologists uncovered an early Anglo-Saxon cremation cemetery, complete with over 300 urns. These weren't your average ash pots — they were handmade, decorated, and bore striking similarities to pottery from Northern Germany and Southern Denmark.

. This strongly suggests that the Angles, one of the Germanic tribes who settled post-Rome, had made Newark their new home.

"Oh, this old urn? Imported. Very continental."

From Pyres to Pews: The Christian Shift

As the centuries rolled on, so did the Christianisation of England. By the 7th century, the old pagan ways were giving way to crosses and cathedrals. In Newark, this shift is shown by the discovery of a Christian burial ground beneath what would later become Newark Castle. Gone were the cremation urns; in came inhumation burials, solemn and sacred. It was a spiritual rebranding — from fiery farewells to peaceful plots, reflecting a society in religious transition.

This wasn't just about burial practices. It marked a broader cultural shift: churches began to appear, literacy spread through monastic centres, and Latin returned — not as the language of empire, but of ecclesiastical authority. Southwell, just down the road, would later become a major ecclesiastical centre, but even in this early period, the seeds of spiritual infrastructure were being sown.

Vikings at the Gate (Literally)

But just as things were settling down, along came the Vikings — not just raiders, but settlers, traders, and cultural influencers. Newark found itself within the Danelaw, the swathe of England under Danish control. And the Norse left their mark — not just in blood and battle, but in language.

Ever wondered why Newark has so many "gates" in its street names? Kirk Gate, Barnby Gate, Carter Gate — it's not about fences. The word "gate" comes from the Old Norse *gata*, meaning "road." So Kirk Gate is the road to the church (*kirkja*), and Barnby Gate? That's Bjarn's road — Named after a Viking settler who knew how to throw a mead-fuelled feast. "Bjarn's Gate? Yeah, that's where the party's at. Just follow the sound of the lyre and the smell of roast boar."

The Norse influence wasn't just linguistic. Place names across the region — like Oxton, Fiskerton, and Thurgarton — bear the hallmarks of Viking settlement. And while Newark may not have been a major Viking stronghold, it was certainly part of the cultural melting pot that defined the Danelaw.

Lady Godiva and the Monastic Mic Drop

As the Saxon era drew to a close, Newark found itself in the hands of none other than Lady Godiva — yes, that Lady Godiva, of naked horse ride fame. Alongside her husband, Leofric, Earl of Mercia, she owned Newark as part of a vast estate portfolio. But in a move that was part piety, part power play, they gifted Newark to the monks at Stow, who in turn passed it on to the Bishops of Lincoln.

This ecclesiastical handover marked the beginning of Newark's religious renaissance. The town would remain under the spiritual and administrative thumb of the bishops for centuries, shaping its development into a market town of regional importance. Because nothing says "divine right" like owning half of Nottinghamshire and having your own mint.

Final Thoughts: Saxon Newark – Fortified, Faithful, and Fiercely Local

The Saxon period was a time of transformation. Newark evolved from a Roman afterthought into a fortified burh, a minting town, a Viking-influenced settlement, and eventually, a monastic stronghold. It was a place where cultures collided, beliefs shifted, and streets were named after Norsemen.

So next time you walk down Bjarn's Gate, remember: you're treading the path of warriors, weavers, monks, and mint-masters. Newark wasn't just surviving the so-called Dark Ages—it was developing, one urn, one coin, and one mead party at a time.

Chapter 6: Castles, Kings, and Market Things – Newark's Medieval Majesty
(1066 AD – 1485 AD)

Featuring a King Who Had a Very Bad Day, and the Origins of Its Walls

The Norman Arrival: Castles, Conquest, and Control

When William the Conqueror landed in 1066 and gave England a rather aggressive Norman makeover, Newark-on-Trent found itself swept up in the grand rebranding of the realm. The Normans weren't just here to rule—they were here to build, fortify, and dominate. And Newark, with its prime location on the River Trent and the ancient Fosse Way, was a strategic gem.

The first Norman castle in Newark was a classic motte and bailey—a quick-build fortress of earth and timber, built atop an early saxon fortification. Think of it as the medieval version of a pop-up stronghold: a big mound (the motte) with a wooden tower on top, surrounded by a fenced courtyard (the bailey). It was William's way of saying, "I'm here, I'm in charge, and I brought my own carpenters." A fine example of this style still exists at Laxton, just up the road, giving us a glimpse of Newark's earliest defences.

By the late 11th century, Newark was roughly the same size as contemporary Nottingham and controlled a vital crossing over the Trent. It was a town on the rise, and the Normans knew it. The castle's location wasn't just scenic—it was strategic. Whoever controlled Newark controlled the river, the road, and the region. And in medieval England, that was the holy trinity of power.

Alexander the Magnificent: Bishop, Builder, and Medieval Mogul

Enter Alexander of Lincoln, the 12th-century bishop who made Newark his personal passion project. Appointed in 1123, Alexander wasn't your average man of the cloth. He was the nephew of Roger of Salisbury, one of King Henry I's top advisors, and he wielded both spiritual and political power with flair.

Alexander was a man of vision—and budget. He expanded Lincoln Cathedral, founded four monasteries, and built castles at Banbury, Sleaford, and, of course, Newark. He was the medieval equivalent of a property tycoon with a divine calling. His contemporaries dubbed him "Alexander the Magnificent," and it's not hard to see why.

In 1135, with England teetering on the brink of civil war (a period known as The Anarchy), Alexander secured royal permission to build a stone castle at Newark. But there was a snag: the Fosse Way ran right through the proposed site. Most people would have built around it. Alexander? He asked the king to move the road. And the king said yes.

Then Alexander asked to build a bridge over the Trent—a massive engineering feat in the 12th century. Again, the king agreed. With the road rerouted and the bridge in place, Newark became a fortified powerhouse and an essential node in England's transport and defence network. It was now officially "The Key to the North"

Its worth mentioning here that Newark is also situated at the Trent's lowest fordable point beneath Hull. Pub quiz fact.... Youre welcome!

King John's Final Stop: Dysentery, Drama, and a Stormy Exit

Fast forward to 1216. England was in chaos. King John, infamous for losing Normandy, clashing with the Church, and being forced to sign (and then ignore) Magna Carta, was on the run. His treasure had just been swallowed by the tides in The Wash—a royal disaster of epic proportions.

Sick with dysentery, exhausted, and politically ruined, John arrived at Newark Castle in October. He died there on the 18th or 19th, during a violent storm that seemed to echo the mess of his reign. Chronicler Matthew Paris later wrote, "Hell is a foul place, made fouler by the presence of King John." Ouch. Though legend says he died in "King John's Tower," historians now believe he expired in the bishop's more comfortable quarters above the gatehouse

. But the story stuck—because let's face it, "King John's Tower" sounds much more dramatic than "That Room Near the Stairs."

The Tunnels of Newark: Fact, Folklore, or Fermented Fantasy?

Ah, the tunnels. Every historic town has them, and Newark is no exception. Tales abound of secret passages linking the castle to pubs, churches, and even other towns. But while Newark does have cellars, vaults, and sally ports, the idea of a vast underground network is more pub talk than engineering reality. Medieval tunnelling was expensive, dangerous, and technically challenging—especially in Newark's sandy, gravelly soil. So while there are certainly intriguing underground spaces, the idea of a mole highway to Nottingham is, sadly, more myth than masonry. Still, it's a great story to tell after your third pint at the Prince Rupert.

The Battle of Lincoln Fair: Knights, Crossbows, and Loot

After John's death, England was still in turmoil. His son, Henry III, was just nine years old, and the French prince Louis had been invited by rebel barons to take the throne. Enter William Marshal, the legendary knight and regent for young Henry. In 1217, Marshal gathered his forces in Newark — 400 knights and 250 crossbowmen — and marched on Lincoln, where French and rebel forces held the castle. The ensuing battle was fierce, chaotic, and decisive. The royalists won, the French fled, and the victors looted the city with gusto.

The event became known as the Battle of Lincoln Fair, a name that perfectly captures the mix of military triumph and medieval shopping spree. Newark, as the staging ground, played a crucial role in saving the English crown — and probably picked up a few bargains in the process

Markets, Fairs, and the Great Wednesday Revolution

While kings and knights made headlines, Newark's real power lay in its marketplace. By the 13th century, it was a bustling commercial hub, thanks to its river, roads, and royal charters. In 1213, Newark made history by petitioning King John to move its market day from Sunday to Wednesday — the first recorded market-day change in England. The reason? Sunday markets were noisy, crowded, and clashed with church services. The king agreed, and Wednesday has been market day ever since. A quiet revolution, but a lasting one.

By the late 13th century, Poll Tax records show Newark had over 1,100 residents — a significant number for the time. It was a bustling, self-sustaining town with a strong economy, a strategic location, and a growing sense of identity
.

Chapter 7: Wool, Wealth, and Winking at the Crown – Tudor Newark's Textile Triumph
(1485 AD – 1603 AD)
Because Fashion Never Dies, and Neither Do Good Inns

A Nation Transformed, and a Town Alongside It

The Tudor period was a time of seismic change in England. From the dynastic victory of Henry VII at the Battle of Bosworth Field in 1485 to the death of Elizabeth I in 1603, the country saw the rise of a centralised monarchy, the dissolution of the monasteries, the birth of the Church of England, and the flowering of the English Renaissance.

While the court was busy with politics, poetry, and the occasional beheading, Newark-on-Trent was quietly weaving its own success story—quite literally.

Newark, nestled on the River Trent and conveniently parked along the Great North Road, was perfectly placed to benefit from the economic and social shifts of the age. While Henry VIII was busy dissolving monasteries and collecting wives, Newark's merchants were collecting wool, weaving cloth, and building fortunes. It was a golden age for trade, textiles, and Tudor-era tax returns.

The Wool Trade: Newark's Golden Thread

By the start of the Tudor era, Newark had already established itself as a regional centre for the wool trade. But under the Tudors, this industry didn't just grow—it boomed. The town's location made it a natural hub for trade. Wool from the surrounding Nottinghamshire countryside—think Southwell, Balderton, and the sheep-strewn fields of Sherwood—was brought into town, processed, dyed, and sold, both locally and abroad.

The town's textile prowess was no accident. As early as the 14th century, Newark had welcomed skilled Flemish weavers, encouraged by royal policy to boost England's cloth production. These artisans brought with them advanced techniques and a flair for quality that helped transform Newark into a centre of textile excellence. By the 16th century, Newark cloth was being exported to the Low Countries, France, and beyond. Somewhere in Bruges, someone was probably wearing a doublet made in Newark and wondering why it smelled faintly of the Trent.

Alan Fleming: Merchant, Magnate, and Monument

One of the most influential figures in Newark's textile history was Alan Fleming, a Flemish merchant who settled in the town in 1339. Though he lived before the Tudor period, his legacy loomed large—literally. His monumental brass in St Mary Magdalene Church is one of the largest Flemish brasses in England, measuring over 9 feet long.

It's not just a memorial; it's a medieval flex. Fleming's trade networks stretched across Europe, and his wealth helped lay the foundations for Newark's later prosperity. He served as bailiff of the town in 1359 and was a generous benefactor to religious causes

His brass, alongside those of fellow drapers John Boston and William Phyllypott, and the chantry chapels of Thomas Meryng and Robert Markham, tells a story of a town built on wool, wealth, and well-placed piety

.

From Raw Wool to Finished Cloth

By the 16th century, Newark's textile industry had evolved from exporting raw wool to producing finished cloth. Fulling mills, which used water power to clean and thicken cloth, were already in operation. The town's drapers and mercers — dealers in cloth and fine fabrics — were doing rather well, and Newark cloth was known for its quality

This shift wasn't just economic; it was social. The growth of the textile industry created jobs, attracted skilled workers, and helped build a prosperous middle class. Newark was no longer just a market town — it was a manufacturing centre. The presence of guilds and trade associations helped regulate quality and maintain Newark's reputation as a producer of fine textiles. And if you were lucky, you might even get a guild dinner out of it — complete with roast swan and a side of civic pride.

Leather, Tanning, and the Scent of Success

Textiles weren't the only game in town. Newark also developed an extensive leather industry. Tanners, saddlers, shoemakers, and glovers all plied their trades in and around the town. The tanning process, which involved soaking hides in vats of urine and other pungent substances, was conducted on the outskirts — far enough from the market to avoid offending delicate noses, but close enough to keep the economy humming.

The leather industry was essential not just for local use but for export. Saddles, boots, gloves, and belts made in Newark found their way to markets across the Midlands and beyond. The industry also supported a network of related trades, from blacksmiths to cobblers. It was a full ecosystem of craftsmanship, commerce, and questionable smells.

Inns, Taverns, and the Art of Hospitality

With trade came travellers, and Newark was ready. The town's inns and taverns were legendary. The Old White Hart Hotel, dating back to 1315, was one of the earliest purpose-built inns in England. It offered food, drink, and lodging to merchants, pilgrims, and the occasional noble on the move.

Other notable establishments included the Saracen's Head — where King Charles I would later spend his final night of freedom — and the Cardinal's Hat (later renamed the Clinton Arms). These weren't just places to sleep — they were centres of social life, where deals were struck, news was exchanged, and ale was consumed in heroic quantities. If walls could talk, these ones would probably slur.

Floods, Bridges, and Bishop Chadworth

In 1457, a devastating flood swept away Newark's bridge over the Trent. Recognising the importance of this crossing, Bishop John Chadworth of Lincoln funded the construction of a new oak bridge, complete with stone towers. It was a vital piece of infrastructure, and a symbol of Newark's resilience and importance.

The bridge not only restored a crucial trade route but also reinforced Newark's role as a regional hub. It connected the town to the wider world and ensured that goods, people, and ideas continued to flow through its streets. And, presumably, kept the sheep moving too.

The Battle of Stoke Field: The Last of the Roses

Just two years into the Tudor era, Newark found itself on the edge of history. In 1487, the Battle of Stoke Field was fought near the village of East Stoke, just outside the town. It was the final battle of the Wars of the Roses, and it ended with the defeat of the Yorkist pretender Lambert Simnel.

Newark, as a nearby settlement, would have seen the movement of troops, the aftermath of battle, and perhaps even the wounded and dying. It was a grim reminder that even in times of prosperity, war was never far away. The battle marked the end of the Plantagenet claim to the throne and solidified Henry VII's hold on power. It also gave Newark a front-row seat to the last medieval punch-up before the Tudors got serious about centralised rule.

A Town of Stone and Spirit

Many of Newark's Tudor-era buildings still stand today. The White Hart Hotel, the Prince Rupert Pub, the Governor's House, and the former Magnus School all date from this period. They are a testament to the town's wealth, its craftsmanship, and its enduring spirit.

St Mary Magdalene Church, with its soaring spire and intricate carvings, was expanded and embellished during the Tudor years. It remains one of the finest parish churches in England — a symbol of Newark's faith, pride, and ambition. The church also houses the tomb of Thomas Magnus, founder of the Magnus School in 1531, a man whose legacy in education still echoes today. He may not have invented the school uniform, but he certainly helped educate the people who would one day wear it.

Conclusion: Threads of Legacy

The Tudor period was a golden age for Newark-on-Trent. It was a time of growth, innovation, and transformation. The town's textile and leather industries flourished. Its inns and markets bustled. Its buildings rose in stone and timber, many of them still standing today.

Newark didn't just survive the upheavals of the Tudor age — it thrived. And in doing so, it wove itself into the fabric of English history, one thread at a time.

Chapter 8: Sieges, Surrender, and Stuart Shenanigans – Newark in the English Civil War (1603 AD – 1714 AD)

It Was Complicated, And Involved a Lot of Digging

The Stuart Ascendancy: A New Dynasty, A Familiar Town

When James VI of Scotland became James I of England in 1603, uniting the crowns of England and Scotland under the Stuart banner, Newark-on-Trent was already a well-established market town with a rich medieval pedigree. Its imposing castle, thriving Wednesday market, and control over both the River Trent and the Great North Road made it a logistical linchpin in the heart of England.

But it was the English Civil War (1642–1651) that would catapult Newark from regional relevance to national notoriety. The town's strategic location made it a prize worth fighting for—and fight they did. Newark became one of the most fiercely contested Royalist strongholds in the country, enduring not one, not two, but three sieges. Think of it as Newark's big break—tragically involving a lot of cannon fire, dysentery and very little sleep.

The English Civil War: Ideologies, Power Struggles, and Religious Tensions

The Civil War was a messy affair. On one side, King Charles I and his Royalist supporters (the Cavaliers), with their flowing locks and fondness for divine right. On the other, Parliament and its Puritan-leaning Roundheads, who preferred short hair, long sermons, and a government that didn't involve royal tantrums.

Newark, with its commanding position on the River Trent and the Great North Road — the A1 of its day — was a critical junction for moving troops, supplies, and messages. Whoever held Newark held the Midlands. And Charles I was not about to let that go without a fight. He visited Newark several times, even using it as a base of operations. The town was loyal to the crown, and the crown, in turn, made Newark a fortress of royal resistance.

Fortifying Newark: Castles, Earthworks, and Ingenious Defences

Newark Castle, originally built in the 12th century by Bishop Alexander of Lincoln, was already a formidable structure But during the Civil War, it became the beating heart of Royalist resistance. Its thick stone walls and riverside position made it a natural fortress.

But the castle alone wasn't enough. Newark's defenders transformed the entire town into a military stronghold. They dug extensive earthworks, constructed ramparts, and built a network of ditches and palisades. The town was ringed with redoubts — small, fortified outposts — each manned by soldiers and bristling with cannon.

The remains of some of these defences can still be traced today, particularly around Queen's Sconce and King's Sconce, two star-shaped earthworks built in 1644 and 1645 respectively. These were Newark's artillery bunkers of their day: geometrically designed to deflect cannonballs and provide overlapping fields of fire. And yes, they're still there — ideal for a Sunday stroll with a side of siege history.

The Sieges of Newark: Resilience and Determination
The First Siege (February 1643)

The first siege was a relatively brief but intense affair. Parliamentarian forces under Major General Thomas Ballard attempted to take the town but were repelled by the Royalist garrison, led by Sir John Henderson.

The defenders had hastily improved Newark's fortifications and were determined to hold their ground. The siege was lifted after just a few days, but it was a warning shot—Newark was now firmly on the war map.

The Second Siege (March 1644)

The second siege was a far more serious undertaking. This time, the Parliamentarians returned with reinforcements—namely, the Scottish Covenanters, led by Sir Joh Meldrum, who had joined the war on Parliament's side. The Royalist defenders, now under the command of Sir Richard Byron (yes, ancestor of the poet Lord Byron), endured months of bombardment and blockade.

The siege was lifted in dramatic fashion by Prince Rupert of the Rhine, King Charles I's dashing nephew and cavalry commander extraordinaire. Rupert, accompanied by his famously bulletproof poodle, Boye, led a daring relief force that broke the siege and sent the Parliamentarians packing. The battle took place near the ruins of St Leonard's Hospice, known as the Spittal, on the east side of the Trent.

It was a personal victory for Rupert and a morale boost for the Royalists. Huzzah

The Third Siege (November 1645 – May 1646)

The third and final siege was the most gruelling. By late 1645, the Royalist cause was collapsing. Newark, now one of the last Royalist strongholds, was surrounded by a massive force of Parliamentarian and Scottish troops. The town was completely cut off. The Scottish Covenanter Army, led by General Alexander Leslie (Earl of Leven), besieged Newark from the north, while Parliamentarian forces under General Sydenham Poyntz (supported by commanders like Colonel Rossiter and Colonel Grey) besieged the town from the south.

The Royalist garrison, led by Lord John Belasyse, held out bravely. But disease and starvation took their toll. Food ran out. Horses were eaten. Morale plummeted. Finally, in May 1646, King Charles I — by then a prisoner of the Scots at Southwell — ordered Newark to surrender. Belasyse complied, and the town fell. The Royalist dream was over, and Newark was left to pick up the pieces. Which was becoming something of the norm.

Life in a Besieged Town: Hardships and Resilience

Life in Newark during the sieges was, in a word, grim. Residents endured constant bombardment, food shortages, and outbreaks of disease. The town's population, which had swelled with Royalist refugees, was crammed into a fortified space with dwindling resources.

Yet the people of Newark showed remarkable resilience. They fortified their homes, shared what little food they had, and supported the Royalist cause with unwavering determination. The town became a hub of wartime logistics, with blacksmiths forging weapons, bakers stretching flour, and apothecaries doing their best with dwindling herbs.

Prices for basic goods skyrocketed. A loaf of bread could cost a week's wages—if you could find one. And yet, through it all, Newark endured. Because if there's one thing Newark does well, it's stubbornness.

The Aftermath: Rebuilding and Remembering

After the war, Newark faced the daunting task of rebuilding. Parliament ordered the town's fortifications dismantled, and Newark Castle was deliberately slighted—partially demolished to prevent future military use. The scars of war were everywhere.

But Newark's spirit remained unbroken. The town gradually recovered. Its market resumed. Trade returned. And in 1660, with the Restoration of the monarchy, Newark once again found its footing.

The legacy of the Civil War remains etched into the town's fabric. Place names like Queen's Sconce and King's Sconce recall the days of siege. The ruins of the castle stand as a monument to Newark's defiance. And the stories—of bravery, hardship, and resilience—are still told today.

Chapter 9: The Georgian Era – Canals, Coaches, and a New Dawn
(1714 AD – 1837 AD)
Finally, Some Peace and Quiet... Kinda. And Fewer Cannons.

A New Dynasty, A New Direction

With the dust of the Civil War long settled and the Stuarts (mostly) out of the picture, the Georgian era dawned with the arrival of the Hanoverians in 1714. King George I, a German-speaking monarch with a fondness for order and a mild confusion about British politics, ushered in a period of relative stability. For Newark-on-Trent, this was a time to breathe, rebuild, and boom.

Gone were the sieges and starvation. In their place came Enlightenment ideals, architectural elegance, and the steady hum of commerce. Newark, already a respected market town, now began to flex its economic and infrastructural muscles in earnest. The town's medieval bones were still visible, but they were being dressed in Georgian finery — lace cuffs, powdered wigs, and all.

Market Day Majesty: The Beating Heart of Newark

Newark's market had been its economic engine for centuries, and in the Georgian era, it roared to life with renewed vigour. The Wednesday market — still a tradition today — was a legacy of a 1213 royal decree by King John, and by the 18th century, it had become a regional magnet for trade.

Farmers from the lush Nottinghamshire countryside brought in livestock, grain, and produce. Artisans sold tools, textiles, and trinkets. The market square buzzed with gossip, haggling, and the occasional goat-related mishap. It wasn't just commerce — it was community. The Market Place, flanked by elegant Georgian buildings, became the town's social and economic nucleus

The River Trent: Newark's Liquid Highway

While the market was Newark's heart, the River Trent was its lifeblood. During the Georgian period, the river underwent a transformation. The 1772 Newark Navigation Act led to major improvements: locks, weirs, and dredging projects that made the Trent more navigable than ever.
Barges, often pulled by horses along towpaths, became the juggernauts of Georgian logistics. They carried coal from Derbyshire, timber from Sherwood, and grain from Lincolnshire. The river connected Newark to the Humber and the North Sea, turning it into a vital inland port.

Two major canal cuts—the Nether Lock Cut and the Cromwell Cut—were constructed to bypass treacherous weirs and shallow bends. These feats of engineering not only improved safety but also sped up trade. The Lock House at Nether Lock, built around 1773, still stands as a charming relic of this watery revolution. It's Newark's answer to a Georgian air traffic control tower—minus the high-vis jackets.

The Great North Road: Coaches, Inns, and the Roar of Hooves

While the river brought goods, the road brought people. The Great North Road, the main route between London and Edinburgh, ran straight through Newark. This made the town a key staging post for stagecoaches, mail coaches, and weary travellers.

About 1770, the road around Newark was raised on a long series of arches to keep it clear of the regular floods—a Georgian workaround for the Trent's occasional tantrums

. Imagine the scene: a coach rattles into town, horses steaming, passengers stretching their legs. Ostlers rush to change the teams, chambermaids prepare rooms, and the innkeeper readies a hearty meal.

Coaching inns like the Saracen's Head (where King Charles I had once stayed) and the Clinton Arms weren't just places to sleep—they were logistical hubs, social centres, and the best places to hear the latest scandal. If you wanted to know who was marrying whom, who was bankrupt, or who had fallen off a horse in Grantham, this was the place.

Georgian Grandeur: Civic Pride and Public Works

The Georgian era wasn't just about trade—it was about transformation. Newark embraced the architectural elegance of the age with gusto. The crown jewel of this civic pride was the Town Hall, completed in 1776 and designed by the renowned architect John Carr of York.

With its classical façade, grand staircase, and elegant ballroom, the Town Hall was more than a building—it was a statement. It housed the Borough Council, hosted court sessions, and served as the venue for glittering social events. If you were anyone in Newark, you attended the mayor's ball. And yes, the wigs were magnificent.

Other public works included the paving of streets, the installation of oil lamps (and later gas lighting), and the construction of new bridges and warehouses. Newark was polishing its image—and its infrastructure. Even the castle grounds was blessed with a makeover, with a large bowling green laid out for the town's more refined citizens

Clean Water and Common Sense

Public health also was gifted a Georgian upgrade. In 1784, Newark installed a public water pump in the Market Place—a small but vital step toward modern sanitation. Before this, residents relied on wells or the river, which, while picturesque, wasn't exactly cholera-free.

The pump was a symbol of progress, a nod to Enlightenment ideals of civic responsibility and public welfare. It also meant fewer people had to drink beer just to avoid dysentery—though let's be honest, many still did. After all, Georgian ale was safer than Georgian water, and considerably more fun.

Brewing, Milling, and Making Things Happen

Newark's economy diversified during the Georgian era. While wool and leather remained important, new industries began to flourish. Flour mills and maltings sprang up, powered by water and wind. Brewing became big business, with Newark ale gaining a reputation for quality (and potency).

Light industry also took root. Small workshops produced everything from tools to textiles. The town's population grew, its streets bustled, and its skyline began to change. Georgian Newark was a town on the move—literally and figuratively. And if you were lucky, you might even get a decent pint and a pair of boots out of it.

A Town in Transition

By the end of the Georgian era, Newark had transformed itself. It was no longer just a market town with a castle and a river. It was a transport hub, an industrial centre, and a community that had embraced the future without forgetting its past.

The scars of war had faded, replaced by the marks of progress: canals, roads, bridges, and buildings that still stand today. Newark had found its rhythm again—steady, confident, and ready for the Victorian age to come.

**Chapter 10: Steam, Sugar, and Social Strife – Newark in the Victorian Era
(1837–1901)**
Cue the Top Hats, Factory Smoke, and Even More Train Whistles!

A New Queen, A New Era, and a Lot More Steam

When 18-year-old Queen Victoria took the throne in 1837, few could have predicted that her reign would stretch over six decades and usher in an age of invention, empire, and industrial oomph. Britain was booming, belching, and building—and Newark-on-Trent was right there in the thick of it, swapping medieval cobbles for modern ambition.

The Victorian era was a paradoxical cocktail of progress and poverty, philanthropy and pollution. It was the age of the penny post, the flush toilet, and the belief that everything—including morals—could be improved with a bit of elbow grease and a lot of coal dust. Newark, with its strategic location on the River Trent and the Great Northern Railway, was perfectly placed to ride the wave of industrialisation—preferably in a top hat and with a firm grip on one's pocket watch.

All Aboard! The Railway Revolution

If the Industrial Revolution had a soundtrack, it was the shriek of a locomotive's whistle—and Newark was soon loudly clattering along. In 1846, the Midland Railway line chugged into town, linking Nottingham to Lincoln and giving Newark its first station. Suddenly, the town was no longer a sleepy market stop—it was a node on the national grid of iron and ambition.

By 1851, the Great Northern Railway mainline from London to York sliced through Newark like a hot knife through butter. Two stations—North Gate and Castle—meant double the hustle, double the bustle, and double the chance of missing your train. The Castle station, with its charming riverside setting, became a gateway for goods and gentry alike.

The railways brought more than just passengers. They brought coal, gypsum, and grain out of Newark, and textiles, tools, and tea in. They brought ideas, fashions, and the occasional Londoner in search of fresh air. And they brought jobs—porters, clerks, engineers, and the all-important tea ladies. Newark was steaming ahead—literally.

Sweet Success: The Sugar Beet Boom

In 1880, Newark got a little sweeter—literally. The Newark Sugar Beet Factory opened its doors and its chimneys, transforming humble root vegetables into refined sugar and the air into a heady mix of steam and syrup.

This wasn't just a factory—it was a symbol of agricultural ingenuity. Instead of importing cane from the Caribbean, Newark's farmers turned their muddy fields into sugar gold. Hundreds were employed, and the town's economy got a much-needed glucose injection. The factory, located near the railway for easy distribution, became a landmark of Victorian industry—and a magnet for wasps.

Brewing, Building, and Plastering the Nation

Newark's traditional trades didn't just survive—they excelled. Brewing was big business, with Warwick & Richardson leading the charge. Their ales were shipped across the country, fuelling everything from pub singalongs to parliamentary debates (probably). The brewery's imposing buildings on Northgate became a symbol of Newark's industrial confidence—and a reliable source of lateness to work on a Monday and questionable decisions.

Meanwhile, Newark's gypsum deposits were being mined and moulded into plaster by the Newark Plaster Company, founded in 1878. If you lived in a Victorian house with smooth walls, chances are Newark had a hand in it. The company's products were shipped far and wide, proving that even humble plaster could be part of the empire-building effort.

Population Boom and the Housing Bust

With industry came people — and lots of them. Newark's population more than doubled, from under 7,000 in 1801 to over 15,000 by 1901. But while the middle classes built gas-lit villas with gardens, the working classes were often crammed into damp, dark terraces.

Sanitation was poor, disease was rife, and cholera was an all-too-frequent visitor. The town's infrastructure groaned under the weight of its own success, and public health reform became a matter of life, death, and politics. The arrival of piped water and proper sewers in the latter half of the century was met with relief — and probably a few celebratory baths.

Social Reform and the Rise of Conscience

The Victorian conscience was a curious beast — equal parts guilt, God, and good intentions. Newark saw a surge in philanthropy, with schools, almshouses, and charities springing up to help the poor help themselves.

Education expanded. Sunday schools taught scripture and spelling. Mechanics' institutes offered lectures on everything from steam engines to Shakespeare. Reading rooms gave workers a place to read, relax, and escape the factory floor—if only for an hour. The Newark Literary and Scientific Institution, founded in 1835, became a hub for self-improvement and polite conversation.

Labour, Leisure, and the Long Road to Rights

Factory life was no picnic. Long hours, low pay, and dangerous machinery were the norm. But the seeds of organised labour were being sown. Workers began to demand better conditions—and slowly, change came.

Leisure also mattered. Football clubs, brass bands, and public parks offered a break from the grind. The Victorians believed in "rational recreation"—fun with a moral purpose. So yes, you could play football, but only if you promised not to swear. The Newark Town Football Club, founded in the 1860s, gave locals a chance to kick something other than a coal bucket.

Civic Pride and the Changing Skyline

Newark's skyline was changing. Church spires and castle ruins were joined by factory chimneys and railway viaducts. But it wasn't all smoke and soot.

The Corn Exchange, the refurbished Town Hall, and new schools reflected a growing sense of civic pride. Streets were paved, gas lamps installed, and sewers (finally!) dug. Newark was becoming a modern town—with all the noise, bustle, and bureaucracy that entailed. The castle grounds were landscaped into a public park and a bowling green—because nothing says Victorian leisure like a well-aimed bowl.

Conclusion: A Town Transformed

By 1901, Newark-on-Trent had been utterly transformed. It was no longer just a medieval market town—it was an industrial powerhouse, a transport hub, and a community grappling with the promises and perils of modernity.

The Victorian era brought steam, sugar, and social change. It brought grime and growth, hardship and hope. And it laid the foundations—quite literally—for the Newark of the 20th century.

Chapter 11: Wars, Waves, and a Changing World – Newark in the 20th Century
(1901–2000)

From "Good Old Days" to "What Just Happened?!" — Now Featuring Accidental Bombings, Council Estates, and the Rise of Retail Parks

A Century of Chaos, Change, and Council Housing

The 20th century didn't politely knock on Newark-on-Trent's door—it kicked it in with muddy boots and a suitcase full of upheaval. From Edwardian elegance to the dawn of the digital age, Newark was swept along by wars, welfare, and Wi-Fi. The town's cobbled streets bore witness to everything from Zeppelin scares to supermarket openings, and its people adapted with grit, humour, and the occasional grumble.

This was a century that began with horse-drawn carts and ended with dial-up internet. Newark, like the rest of Britain, had to learn to navigate two world wars, a housing crisis, the rise of the motorcar, and the existential threat of the out-of-town retail park. And somehow, it did.

The Great War: Sacrifice and Service

In 1914, Newark was still a town of gas lamps, horse-drawn carts, and a market square that hadn't changed a great deal… oh.. other than the Georgian remodeling. But the First World War brought seismic shifts. Hundreds of Newark men enlisted, many joining the Sherwood Foresters. The town's industries—brewing, plaster, and engineering—pivoted to support the war effort.

Newark became a training ground and a place of healing. The Magnus Grammar School was requisitioned as a hospital, and the town's churches and halls hosted fundraisers, knitting circles, and recruitment drives. Women stepped into roles previously reserved for men, working in munitions at Worthington & Simpsons, uniforms at Mumby & Sons, and parachutes at Coopers.

The war left deep scars—memorials like the one in the Market Place became permanent reminders of sacrifice. The Ransome & Marles memorial plaque still stands as a tribute to the workers who never came home.

Between the Wars: Industry, Innovation, and Interwar Blues

The 1920s brought jazz, flappers, and a brief economic boom. Newark's engineering firms, especially Ransome & Marles, expanded their output. The plaster industry, fuelled by local gypsum, kept the town dusty and employed. Brewing remained a source of both income and hangovers.

But the 1930s brought the Great Depression. Unemployment rose, soup kitchens appeared, and political tensions simmered. The rise of the motorcar began to reshape Newark's roads and rhythms. The town's first bus services began, and the railway's dominance began to wane. Still, Newark soldiered on—because that's what Newark does.

World War II: Bombs, Bombers, and Blackouts

When war returned in 1939, Newark was more prepared—but still vulnerable.

Manufacturing Might

Ransome & Marles became a key supplier of ball bearings, essential for aircraft, tanks, and naval gun turrets. The factory ran day and night, and its workers—many of them women—became the town's unsung heroes. The Ransome Brass Band, formed in 1937, even broadcast live from the works canteen to boost morale.

RAF Winthorpe

Constructed in 1940, RAF Winthorpe became a major Bomber Command base. Lancasters and Halifaxes thundered overhead, and the airfield buzzed with activity. Newarkers watched the skies with pride and fear, knowing not all planes would return. After the war, the site became home to the Newark Air Museum—because if you're going to have a runway, you might as well fill it with vintage aircraft.

The Ransome and Marles Bombing

On 7 March 1941, Newark experienced its "Blackest Day." Two German planes bombed the Ransome & Marles factory, killing 41 people and injuring 165 more. The attack was swift and brutal—bombs hit the works, the shelter, and even machine-gunned the site. The factory was so vital it was rebuilt in just three weeks
Newark didn't just mourn—it got back to work.

POWs and Post-War Ploughshares

After the war, RAF Winthorpe became a prisoner-of-war camp. Many German POWs stayed on, working on farms and even marrying locals. Their legacy lives on in surnames, stories, and a few surprisingly good bratwurst recipes.

Post-War Rebuilding: Bricks, Buses, and Bureaucracy

The post-war years were about rebuilding—physically, emotionally, and economically. Council estates like Hawtonville sprang up to house returning soldiers and growing families. Victorian terraces were modernised, and new schools, clinics, and community centres appeared.

The town's economy diversified. While plaster and brewing remained, light manufacturing, retail, and services took centre stage. The arrival of supermarkets and chain stores changed shopping habits forever. Newark was no longer just a market town—it was a regional hub. And yes, the queues at the new Co-op were legendary.

The Swinging Sixties (and the Slightly Less Swinging Seventies)

The 1960s brought pop music, miniskirts, and the A1 bypass (1964), which diverted traffic from the town centre and changed the character of the Great North Road. The town embraced modernity—cautiously. The bypass was a blessing for congestion and a curse for footfall.

In 1974, the Newark and Sherwood District Council was formed, consolidating local governance and ushering in an era of planning permissions, paperwork, and the occasional pothole. Civic pride remained strong, even if the paperwork multiplied. And somewhere in a filing cabinet, a plan for a leisure centre was probably gathering dust.

Late Century: Decline, Diversification, and Digital Dawn

The 1980s and 90s saw the decline of traditional industries. Deindustrialisation hit Newark, as it did much of Britain. But the town adapted. Tourism grew, with renewed interest in Newark Castle, St Mary Magdalene Church, and the town's Civil War history. The National Civil War Centre was still a twinkle in a curator's eye, but the seeds were being sown.

Retail flourished. National chains arrived. Leisure centres were built. The town centre was pedestrianised. Newark was changing — but it hadn't forgotten its roots. The past was still present — in the architecture, the street names, and the stories passed down in pubs.

Conclusion: A Town Transformed

By 2000, Newark-on-Trent had weathered wars, economic shifts, and technological revolutions. It had grown, adapted, and thrived. The 20th century brought bombs and bureaucracy, hardship and hope — and laid the foundations for the Newark of the 21st century.

It wasn't always easy. But then again, Newark never asked for easy. It asked for resilience, resourcefulness, and the occasional brass band. And it got all three.

Chapter 12: Renaissance, Revival, and the Digital Age – Newark in the 21st Century

(2000–Present Day)
Where Ancient History Meets Wi-Fi, and the Locals Still Love a Good Market Day

A New Millennium, A Familiar Market

As the 21st century dawned, Newark-on-Trent found itself at a curious intersection—where cobbled lanes met fibre-optic cables, and where the scent of artisan sourdough mingled with the faint whiff of nostalgia. The town, with its medieval street plan and the ever-watchful gaze of Newark Castle, wasn't just clinging to the past—it was giving it a cheeky wink while striding into the future in sensible shoes.

The Wednesday and Saturday markets remained the town's beating heart, pulsing with the energy of stallholders who could sell you a wedge of Stilton, a vinyl copy of *Bat Out of Hell*, and a conspiracy theory—all before your second coffee. The Buttermarket buzzed with chatter, gossip, and the occasional heated debate over the best sausage roll in Nottinghamshire (spoiler: it's still under investigation).

And if you wandered too far, you might find yourself in the antiques section, where every item had a story, and most of them involved ghosts.

Heritage and High-Speed Internet

Newark's love affair with history took a bold leap forward in 2015 with the opening of the National Civil War Centre. Housed in the lovingly restored Magnus School building, it became the town's answer to Hogwarts—if Hogwarts had more muskets and fewer owls. Visitors were treated to immersive exhibits, costumed guides who took their roles *very* seriously, and a gift shop where you could buy a pike, a pamphlet, and a Civil War-themed tea towel that read "Keep Calm and Reload."

But while Newark was busy reenacting the 1640s, it was also quietly becoming a digital dynamo. High-speed broadband swept through the town faster than a rumour at the Castle Barge. Suddenly, Sherwood's finest were Zooming, streaming, and launching Etsy empires from their conservatories. Even the pigeons in the Market Place seemed to be syncing with the cloud.

The River Reimagined

The River Trent, once Newark's industrial lifeline, underwent a glow-up worthy of a Channel 4 makeover show. Gone were the coal barges and clanking cranes—replaced by paddleboarders, prosecco picnics, and the occasional swan-related standoff. The riverside became a haven for joggers, dog walkers, and people pretending to jog while actually looking for ice cream.

The Newark Festival turned the waterfront into a summer spectacle, with live music, food stalls, and fireworks that startled every cat from Balderton to Farndon. One year, a tribute act called "Elvis Parsley" stole the show—and a few hearts. The river, once a highway for timber and toil, now carried laughter, inflatable flamingos, and the occasional confused canoeist from Lincoln.

Retail, Resilience, and Reinvention

While high streets across the UK were having an existential crisis, Newark's town centre held its own with a stiff upper lip and a strong flat white. Yes, some big-name chains packed up their tills and left, but the independents stood firm. From the bookshop that smelled like wisdom and biscuits, to the chocolatier that turned truffles into an art form, Newark's shops were as quirky as they were resilient.

Then came 2020. The pandemic hit like a rogue shopping trolley in Asda's car park. Streets emptied, shutters came down, and the town held its breath. But Newark rallied. Volunteers delivered essentials, businesses went digital overnight, and Zoom quizzes became the new pub crawl. The town's centuries-old spirit of community kicked in—because if there's one thing Newark knows, it's how to survive a siege.

Sustainability and Smart Growth

As the world turned its gaze to greener pastures, Newark and Sherwood rolled up their sleeves and got planting. Sconce and Devon Park became not just a green lung for the town, but a social hub for dog walkers, tai chi enthusiasts, and teenagers pretending not to be on TikTok. New cycle paths appeared like magic (or council funding), and walking trails encouraged locals to rediscover the joys of not driving to the Co-op.

The Middlebeck development rose from the fields like a sustainable phoenix—complete with energy-efficient homes, green corridors, and archaeological digs that unearthed yet more Roman pottery (because Newark can't dig a hole without finding a bit of empire). Growth here wasn't about sprawl—it was about smart planning, community voices, and making sure the new houses didn't block anyone's view of the castle.

Looking Ahead

As Newark-on-Trent marches into the future, it does so with a swagger born of centuries of reinvention. It's a town where you can buy a medieval-style pork pie, pay with contactless, and post a selfie with it in front of the castle—all before your bus to Southwell arrives (late, but with charm).

It's a place that's been besieged, bombed, bypassed, and occasionally baffled by its own one-way system—but it always bounces back. And as long as there's a market on Wednesday, a festival in summer, and someone in the pub who remembers when the river froze in '63, Newark will keep doing what it does best; Adapting, and telling its story—one witty, wonderful chapter at a time.

Still Standing, Still Selling, Still Slightly Sarcastic (and Proud of It)

And so we arrive at the final page—for now—of Newark-on-Trent's ever-evolving story. A town that's weathered the centuries with grit, grace, and just the right amount of cheek. From the ancient flint-knappers of Farndon Fields to the broadband-boosted baristas of Middlebeck, Newark has never been content to simply exist. It thrives. It adapts. It laughs in the face of adversity—and then probably writes a witty Facebook post about it.

This is a town that's been invaded by Vikings, besieged during the Civil War, bombed in the Blitz, and occasionally confused by its own one-way system. It's hosted monarchs, mourned martyrs, and brewed enough ale to keep the Trent wet. And yet, through every twist of history, Newark has done what it does best: kept calm, carried on, and made sure the Wednesday market opened on time.

But Newark is more than its history. It's the people who make it pulse. The stallholders who know your name and your favourite cheese. The volunteers who show up when it matters most. The teachers, the traders, the teens on scooters, the pensioners with stories that could fill a library. It's the laughter echoing through the Market Place, the quiet pride in a well-kept garden, the shared nod between strangers who both remember when the river froze.

So next time you stroll past the castle walls or dodge a particularly ambitious pigeon near the Buttermarket, take a moment. You're not just walking through a town—you're walking through centuries of resilience, reinvention, and relentless charm. Newark isn't just a postcode. It's a patchwork of people, places, and pride stitched together with humour and heart.

Thanks for coming along for the ride. Now go—tell your friends, share the stories, and maybe—just maybe—treat yourself to a Civil War-themed tea towel. Because if any town deserves a bit of merch, it's this one.
Newark-on-Trent: still standing, still selling, and still absolutely brilliant

Special Treats
:)

Newark-on-Trent: A Brief History with Extra Sass:

Condensed TimeLine

14,000 BC – 10,000 BC: The Original Flintstones
Cavemen rocked up with flint tools and a dream. Farndon Fields was the prehistoric hotspot for hunting mammoths and red deer. Basically, Newark was the Stone Age's version of Center Parcs.

10,000 – 3300 BC: From Spears to Spades
Mesolithic folks brought tiny arrow bits (microliths), then Neolithic types said, "Let's settle down," invented farming, and started the first allotments (just not in Newark). One axe even got recycled into a whetstone. Eco-warriors before it was cool.

3300 – 700 BC: Bronze Age Bling
Middlebeck revealed a henge (prehistoric VIP lounge), 35 cremation burials, and a polished axe from Cumbria. Clearly, Newark was the place to be buried and accessorised.

800 BC – 43 AD: Iron Age Swag
The Corieltauvi tribe farmed, forged, and flaunted gold torcs. Newark's Iron Age residents had roundhouses, loom weights, and serious jewellery game. The Newark Torc? Total Iron Age haute couture.

43 – 410 AD: Romans: Pottery, Please
Newark didn't get a Roman name (rude), but it did get 73 pottery kilns. That's not a hobby, that's a full-blown ceramic empire. Also: beer, villas, and a dodecahedron. Because why not?

410 – 1066 AD: Saxons, Vikings & Lady Godiva
Newark became a "burh" (fortified town), minted coins, and hosted over 300 urns. Street names like "Barnby Gate" come from Norse. Oh, and Lady Godiva owned the place. Yes, that Lady Godiva.

1066 – 1485 AD: Medieval Mayhem
Newark Castle was built, King John died here (with dysentery, no less), and the town got its market moved to Wednesday. Also: knights, fairs, and a battle called "Lincoln Fair" (yes, really).

1485 – 1603 AD: Tudor Textiles & Tavern Tales
Wool was king. Flemish weavers made Newark the Milan of medieval England. Inns popped up, floods knocked down bridges, and just outside town, The Battle of Stoke Field ended the Wars of the Roses.

1603 – 1714 AD: Stuart Shenanigans
Newark was besieged THREE (yes, Three, Tres, Trois, Drei, Tre) times during the Civil War. The castle held strong but eventually surrendered when King Charles I said "enough." Locals endured cannonballs, starvation, and probably some very bad hair days.

1714 – 1837 AD: Georgian Glow-Up
Brick buildings, posh coffee houses, and Enlightenment chit-chat. Newark got stylish, intellectual, and slightly smug. The Town Hall and Market thrived, and beer was still a major food group.

1837 – 1901 AD: Victorian Vibes
Trains arrived, factories boomed, and Newark ironworks made everything from bearings to banisters. Sanitation improved (finally), and the town got a proper glow-up with Gothic spires and civic pride.

1900s: Wars, Floods & Rock 'n' Roll
Two world wars, a factory bombing, and a royal visit. Newark powered through with grit, jazz, and a lot of tea. The 1960s brought dance halls, denim, and dreams of the future.

2000s: Digital Newark & Facebook Fame
Newark entered the 21st century with broadband, baristas, and a booming photo group. The Civil War Centre opened, glamping took off, and the town's quirks went viral. History, meet hashtags.

The Historic Buildings of Newark

Newark-on-Trent is home to a remarkable collection of over 360 listed buildings, each telling a story of the town's rich and layered history. Here's a curated list of some of the most historically significant buildings, along with their approximate dates of construction:

.

This is just a glimpse into Newark's architectural heritage. www.newarkguide.co.uk includes everything from former maltings and breweries to telephone kiosks and war memorials.

Interactive map

All of the following buildings and historic sites can be found on the interactive map (which has over 250 plotted historic sites that you can visit)

https://www.newarkguide.co.uk/interactive-map

Newark Castle

Once a medieval fortress, now a picturesque riverside ruin, Newark Castle was built in the 12th century by Bishop Alexander of Lincoln. It played a starring role in the English Civil War as a Royalist stronghold and endured multiple sieges. Today, it's more about picnics than pikes, with tranquil gardens and dramatic views that make it a favourite for history buffs and romantics alike. Newark Castle saw many English Knights Templar imprisoned in its dungeons interrogated and tortured after the order was suppressed in 1307

St Mary Magdalene Church

This 12th-century marvel boasts one of the tallest spires in Nottinghamshire and some of the finest stained glass this side of Canterbury. It's been a spiritual and architectural beacon for centuries, and if you listen closely, you might just hear the echoes of medieval choirs — or the creak of tourists craning their necks.

The Governors House

A fine example of 15th-century timber-framed architecture, this grand residence once housed the governor of Newark Castle. Now privately owned, it's a reminder that even in the days of powdered wigs and quill pens, real estate was all about location.

The Ossington

Built in the 19th century by Lady Ossington to promote temperance (read: no booze. Ironically, the money for the temperance project came from her husband, who make a fortune from brewing. Pub quiz gold that is!). This grand building ironically now serves as a pub. Proof that even the most sober intentions can lead to a good pint and a great night out.

Moot Hall
This 15th-century timber-framed gem once served as Newark's courthouse. Justice was swift, and probably a bit drafty. Today, it's a striking reminder of the town's medieval roots and a favourite photo op for lovers of crooked beams and straight history.

The Town Lock
A working lock on the River Trent, this piece of 18th-century engineering is where Newark's industrial past meets its leisurely present. Watch narrowboats glide through and marvel at the fact that water traffic still requires more patience than the M1.

The Prince Rupert
Named after the dashing Royalist commander, this 16th-century pub oozes character—and probably a few ghost stories. With its low beams and roaring fires, it's the perfect place to toast to history (and maybe a second round).

Old White Hart
A former coaching inn dating back to the 16th century, the Old White Hart once welcomed weary travellers and their horses.

The Corn Exchange
Built in the 19th century for trading grain, this grand building now hosts events, performances, and the occasional wedding It's a place where commerce once reigned.

The Friary
Founded in the 13th century, this former Franciscan friary is now a peaceful retreat. Once home to monks and their meditations, it's now a haven for quiet contemplation and the occasional squirrel.

Newark Violin School
Housed in a handsome Victorian building, this internationally renowned school is where violins are crafted and played with equal finesse. It's the only place where being strung out is a compliment.

Former Toll House
This tiny 18th-century building once collected tolls from travellers—proof that even back then, the road to anywhere came with a fee. Now it's a quaint reminder of Newark's transport history.

National Civil War Museum
Located in the heart of Newark, this museum dives deep into one of Britain's most chaotic chapters. Expect swords, sieges, and stories galore—plus a gift shop that's thankfully less bloody.

The Gilstrap Centre
Originally a library, this elegant Victorian building is a local landmark. With its arched windows and civic pride, it's a place where history meets helpfulness.

22–24 Kirkgate
These beautifully preserved medieval buildings are a rare glimpse into Newark's architectural past. If walls could talk, these would probably whisper in Middle English.

Newark Town Hall
Built in the 18th century, this grand civic building is where Newark's big decisions are made—and where chandeliers outnumber spreadsheets. It's as elegant as it is important.

Kirkgate Cottages
These charming 18th-century cottages are the kind of place you'd expect to find a bonneted heroine or a chimney sweep. Delightfully preserved and full of character.

Old Magnus Grammar
Founded in 1529, this historic school has educated generations of Newark's finest. Its stone walls have seen centuries of learning—and probably a few ink-stained fingers.

Lock Keepers Cottage
This riverside cottage once housed the person responsible for keeping the boats moving. Quaint, cosy, and perfectly placed for watching the world (and the water) go by.

The Palace Theatre
Opened in 1920, this Art Deco gem is Newark's cultural crown jewel. From Shakespeare to stand-up, it's where the town comes to be entertained—and occasionally enlightened.

The Queens Head
Serving pints since the 16th century, this historic pub is where locals gather, stories are swapped, and the beer flows like history itself.

Newark's Thinnest House
At just over six feet wide, this quirky little home proves that you don't need much space to make a big impression. It's the architectural equivalent of a tight squeeze.

Old Bakery Tea Room
Once a bakery, now a tea room, this cosy spot is perfect for a cuppa and a slice of something sweet. It's where carbs and comfort collide.

Trent Bridge
Spanning the River Trent, this historic bridge has carried carts, cars, and countless conversations. A scenic stroll with a side of history.

GuildHall
While the original medieval Guildhall no longer stands, its legacy is preserved in the town's layout and historical records. It was closely associated with the town's merchant guilds and civic leaders, and would have been a hub for decision-making, trade regulation, and community events.

Former Factories

Trent Navigation Wharf

The Trent Navigation Company was established by an Act of Parliament in 1783 to improve and maintain navigation on the River Trent. The company was responsible for constructing towpaths and other infrastructure to facilitate the movement of goods along the river. Newark, with its strategic location, became a key point for these activities.

The Trent Navigation Wharf in Newark included warehouses and other facilities designed to support the loading and unloading of goods. These structures were built to accommodate the needs of river transport, with robust construction to withstand the demands of industrial use.

The wharf played a crucial role in Newark's economy, serving as a hub for the transportation of goods such as coal, grain, and other commodities. The improvements made by the Trent Navigation Company helped to boost trade and commerce in the region. The wharf was part of a broader network of waterways that connected Newark to other major industrial centers.

Today, the legacy of Trent Navigation Wharf is remembered as part of Newark's rich industrial heritage. While the original structures may no longer be in use, the site remains a point of historical interest, reflecting the town's past as a bustling center of river-based trade.

Castle Brewery

Castle Brewery was established in 1885 by the brewers Caparne & Hankey. The brewery was designed by the renowned architect William Bradford, known for his work on brewery buildings. The brewery's location in Newark was strategic, taking advantage of the town's transportation links and industrial infrastructure.

The brewery complex is a Grade II listed site, reflecting its architectural and historical significance. The buildings were constructed in a French Renaissance style, characterized by ornate detailing and robust brickwork2. Notable features include the brewery tower, which remains a prominent landmark in Newark

Castle Brewery played a significant role in Newark's brewing industry. It produced a variety of beers and ales, contributing to the town's reputation for high-quality brewing1. The brewery operated successfully for nearly a century, becoming an integral part of the local economy and community.

The brewery ceased operations in 1982. Since then, the site has been redeveloped into a mixed-use complex, including residential and commercial spaces1. The redevelopment has preserved many of the original architectural features, maintaining the historical character of the site while adapting it for modern use.

Former Gypsum Grinding Mill

The gypsum grinding mill was established to process gypsum, a mineral used in various industries, including construction and agriculture. Newark's location near significant gypsum deposits made it an ideal site for such a facility.

The mill was designed to accommodate the grinding and processing of gypsum. It featured robust industrial architecture typical of the late 19th and early 20th centuries, with large storage areas and machinery for grinding the mineral into a fine powder. The building's design was functional, focusing on efficiency and durability.

Gypsum processing was an important industry in Newark, contributing to the local economy and providing employment for many residents. The mill played a crucial role in supplying gypsum for various uses, including plaster and fertilizer production. Its operation was integral to the town's industrial landscape.

Warwick Brewery

Warwick Brewery was founded by Samuel Sketchley at the Tower Wharf Brewery in 17661. In 1856, Richard Warwick acquired the brewery, marking the beginning of its significant expansion1. The Northgate Brewery, where Warwick Brewery was located, was built in 1871.

The brewery complex included several notable buildings, such as the Northgate Brewery Office Range and Brewhouse, which are listed on the Historic England website. The architecture of these buildings reflects the industrial style of the late 19th century, with robust brickwork and functional design elements suited to brewing operations.

Warwick Brewery played a crucial role in Newark's brewing industry. In 1888, the brewery merged with Richardson, Earp & Slater's Trent Brewery to form Warwicks and Richardson's Ltd. This merger allowed the company to expand its operations and increase its market presence. The brewery produced a variety of beers and ales, which were distributed widely.

In 1962, Warwick Brewery was acquired by John Smith's Tadcaster Brewery Co. Ltd., and brewing operations ceased in 19661. Despite the closure, many of the original buildings remain standing and have been repurposed for residential and commercial use1. The brewery's legacy continues to be remembered as an integral part of Newark's industrial heritage.

Thorpes Warehouse

Thorpe's Warehouse, located on Millgate, was built in 1872 as a riverside barley store and malt house[1]. Its strategic location along the River Trent facilitated the transportation of goods, making it an important part of Newark's industrial landscape. The warehouse is a Grade II listed building, reflecting its architectural and historical significance[1]. The structure features traditional 19th-century industrial design elements, including robust brickwork and large storage spaces. The east-facing elevation of the building is particularly notable for its historical character.

In 1932, the premises were acquired by Newark Egg Packers Ltd., and the building was converted from a malt house to a warehouse[1]. This transition marked a new phase in its use, adapting to the changing industrial needs of the area. Later, in the 1980s or early 1990s, the building was rented out to Weston Mill Pottery.

The warehouse lay vacant between 2007 and 2010 until planning permission was granted in 2011 for its restoration and conversion into high-quality commercial suites and residential apartments. The project was completed around 2013 or 2014, with the original hand-painted inscription "Thorpe's Warehouse" restored[1]. Today, it comprises 12 luxury apartments, blending modern living with historical charm.

Strays Windmill

Stray's Windmill was first recorded on maps in 1825. It was one of several windmills in the Newark area, reflecting the town's agricultural heritage. Windmills were essential for grinding grain into flour, a crucial process for local food production.

The windmill was a traditional tower mill, a common design in the 19th century. Tower mills are characterized by their tall, cylindrical structures made of brick or stone, with a rotating cap that allows the sails to turn into the wind1. Stray's Windmill would have featured these typical elements, although specific architectural details are less documented.

Located between Newark and Farndon

Nicholsons Factory

Nicholson's factories in Newark-on-Trent, particularly the Trent Ironworks, have a storied history that reflects the town's industrial heritage.

Nicholson's Iron Foundry was established by Benjamin Nicholson, who was born in South Carlton near Lincoln in 1785. By 1809, he had moved to Newark and started trading as a partner in Nicholson, Bemrose & Co., retail ironmongers. In 1820, he entered the wholesale iron business, and by 1825, he had opened a foundry for manufacturing cast-iron domestic goods.

The Trent Ironworks, located along the River Trent, was ideally situated for industrial operations. The site included a wharf beside the river and sidings onto the Midland Railway's Nottingham to Lincoln line, facilitating the efficient receipt of raw materials and dispatch of finished products1. The foundry's distinctive clock-tower, which housed the drawing offices, managers' offices, and clerks' department, remains a prominent landmark in Newark.

Coopers Dressing Gown Factory

Cooper's Dressing Gown Factory was established in 1894 on Victoria Street. The factory was known for producing a wide range of garments, but it became particularly famous for its quilted dressing gowns[1]. The business originally started with the production of workmen's shirts in the early 19th century by the owner of Freeman's Drapery Warehouse[1]. As demand grew, the factory expanded its product line to include women's wear such as tea gowns and underclothes, styled to the latest French designs.

The factory was purpose-built to accommodate the growing business. It featured modern facilities for the time and was designed to maximize production efficiency. The building's architecture reflected the industrial style of the late 19th century, with functional design elements suited to garment manufacturing.

Victoria Street, Newark

Mills Warehouse

Mills Warehouse in Newark-on-Trent is a historic building located along the River Trent. Originally a 19th-century industrial mill, it has recently been the focus of redevelopment efforts to transform it into residential apartments.

The warehouse played a significant role in Newark's industrial past, contributing to the town's economic growth during the 19th century. Its location by the river was strategic for transporting goods

Town Wharf Brewery

The Town Wharf Brewery, originally known as Handley and Sketchley's Town Wharf Brewery, was established around 1766. Samuel Sketchley, who learned his craft in Burton-on-Trent, partnered with William Handley, a local banker. This partnership marked the beginning of large-scale commercial brewing in Newark.
The brewery was strategically located near the River Trent, which was crucial for transporting goods. The site included warehouses and wharves, allowing for efficient distribution of ale

.The building's design was influenced by its function as a transport interchange, facilitating the movement of goods by both land and water

The Wharf, Newark

Former Warwick Maltings

The former Warwick Maltings in Newark-on-Trent, also known as the Warwick and Richardson's Brewery malt house, is a significant historical building with a rich past.

The malt house was constructed in 1864 by Warwick and Richardson's Brewery[1]. The building was made using bricks from the Cafferata company at Beacon Hill and ironwork supplied by the Trent Ironworks of W.N. Nicholson & Sons[1]. This construction reflects the industrial growth and architectural style of the period.

The malt house is a three-storey building with a basement, built of red brick with yellow brick dressings[1]. It features gabled and hipped slate roofs, which are characteristic of the industrial architecture of the 19th century[1]. The building's design includes a date stone on the northeast gable inscribed with "P W Archt. 1864"

Historic Points of Interest

Civil War Statue

Located outside the Ossington, the Civil War statue is a prominent monument that commemorates Newark's significant role during the English Civil War. The statue depicts a Royalist soldier, symbolizing the town's steadfast loyalty to King Charles I during the three sieges between 1643 and 1646. Erected in 1988, and moved to its current location recently, the statue serves as a reminder of Newark's turbulent past and its strategic importance during one of England's most tumultuous periods.

The Town Pump

The Newark Town Pump, situated in the Market Place, is a historic landmark dating back to the 18th century. Originally installed to provide a reliable source of clean water for the town's residents, the cast-iron pump features ornate detailing typical of the period's craftsmanship. Although no longer in use, the town pump remains a cherished part of Newark's historical landscape, reflecting the town's development and the importance of public utilities in urban life.

Beaumond Cross

Beaumond Cross, located in the Library Gardens, is a historic monument with a rich history dating back to the medieval period. Believed to have been erected in the late 13th or early 14th century during the reign of Edward III, the cross is a fine example of Edwardian English Gothic architecture. Despite weathering and the passage of time, the Beaumond Cross remains a well-preserved and significant landmark in Newark, reflecting the town's medieval heritage and architectural history.

Queen Sconce Statue

The Civil War statue on Queen's Sconce in Sconce Park is a notable monument commemorating Newark's role during the English Civil War. The statue, a latticework cannon, honors the Royalist forces who defended Newark during the sieges from 1643 to 1646. The Queen's Sconce itself is a well-preserved earthwork fortification named after Queen Henrietta Maria, the wife of King Charles I. This site serves as an educational and historical landmark, attracting visitors interested in Newark's Civil War heritage.

Ironmonger Row & The Church Chimney

Ironmonger Row is a historic street that reflects Newark's rich commercial heritage. Once home to numerous ironmongers and related trades, the street is lined with buildings showcasing a mix of architectural styles. The church chimney near St. Mary Magdalene Church, built in 1854, served the church's heating boiler. Preserved by the Newark Local History Society, the chimney reflects its significance as part of the church's infrastructure and the broader historical landscape of Newark.

Lord Byron's Poems

A plaque commemorating Lord Byron's poems is located on the outside of G.H. Porters at the corner of Market Place and Ridge Street. It marks the spot where S. and J. Ridge, a local printing firm, published Byron's first volumes of poetry, "Fugitive Pieces" in November 1806 and "Hours of Idleness" in July 1807. This plaque highlights Newark's connection to the famous Romantic poet and celebrates the town's literary heritage.

Cannonball Hole

The cannonball hole in the spire of St. Mary Magdalene Church is a poignant reminder of Newark's turbulent history during the English Civil War. The church tower served as a lookout point for the Royalist garrison during the sieges of Newark. In 1644, a Parliamentarian cannonball struck the spire, leaving a visible hole that remains to this day. This historical scar is part of the Civil War Trail in Newark, highlighting the town's strategic importance and the fierce battles that took place there.

Chain Lane

Chain Lane is a historic street that reflects Newark's rich architectural and commercial heritage. Home to several Grade II listed buildings dating back to the 18th and 19th centuries, the lane showcases traditional brick construction and period architectural details. Chain Lane has long been a part of Newark's bustling town center, blending historical charm with modern amenities.

Cuckstool Wharf

Cuckstool Wharf, located along Castle Gate, dates back to the Stuart period and was used extensively during the Victorian era. The wharf served as a key point for loading and unloading goods transported via the River Trent, contributing significantly to Newark's commercial activity. Although now disused, Cuckstool Wharf remains an important part of the town's industrial heritage.

Smeaton's Arches
. Built to carry the Great North Road across the floodplain of the River Trent, the arches ensured the road remained passable during floods. Today, 74 of the original 125 arches remain, reflecting their historical and architectural significance as a Grade II listed structure.

Romanesque Arch
The Romanesque Arch, located in the Gilstrap Centre, is an elaborately carved structure believed to have been the entrance to a chapel within Newark Castle. Erected by the Friends of Newark Castle in 2009, the arch is thought to have been unearthed in the Castle Grounds or recovered from the river. It lay in the Castle undercroft for some 50 years before being restored and displayed.

Fountain Gardens
Fountain Gardens, a charming public park dating back to the Victorian era, features a central fountain, well-maintained flower beds, pathways, and seating areas. The gardens provide a tranquil green space for residents and visitors, reflecting Newark's commitment to preserving its historical and recreational spaces.

Longstone Bridge
Longstone Bridge, built in 1819 for the Newark Navigation Company, is a Grade II listed structure that carries the towpath over a side channel of the River Trent. Constructed from ashlar stone, the bridge played a crucial role in facilitating river navigation and trade during the 19th century, contributing to Newark's economic development.

Odinist Temple

The Newark Odinist Temple, consecrated on Midsummer's Day in 2014, is the first heathen temple in England in over a thousand years. Located in a Grade II listed building dating from the Tudor period, the temple was originally an almshouse chapel known as the Bedehouse Chapel. Restored by the Odinist Fellowship, the temple now serves as a place of worship for Odinists, featuring specially commissioned paintings and historic architecture.

Coach and Horses Passage

Coach and Horses Passage, a historic alleyway running from Castle Gate to Middle Gate, is named after the Coach and Horses Inn. The passage features a unique low, sloping, grooved projection installed in 1846 to deter men from relieving themselves against the passage wall. Today, it serves as a charming reminder of Newark's past.

Sibthorpe Dovecote

Located a short distance from Newark, the Sibthorpe Dovecote dates back to 1370. This solitary structure, resembling a disused windmill or a fairytale prison cell, housed over 1,200 pigeons in tiny nesting niches. Built by monks in response to a famine in 1360, the dovecote provided an unlimited supply of meat, eggs, and fertilizer. Now a Grade I listed building, the dovecote is owned by Nottinghamshire County Council.

Otter Park

Otter Park, a small public park located on Millgate, features a central sculpture of two bronze otters created by artist Judith Bluck around 2009-2010. The park offers a peaceful green space for residents and visitors, forming part of Newark's Riverside Walk.

Duke of Wellington Yard

Duke of Wellington Yard, named after the famous British soldier and statesman, was formerly the site of the Duke of Wellington Inn. The yard and its surrounding structures reflect Newark's rich architectural heritage and its evolution from a bustling market town to a modern urban center.

Jubilee Arch

Commissioned by the town council to mark the Queen's Golden Jubilee in 2002, the Jubilee Arch stands as a testament to Newark's celebration of significant national events.

Millennium Monument

The Millennium Monument, unveiled in 2000 to mark the turn of the millennium, is a striking sculpture located in the Market Place. The monument features a contemporary design with a central column surrounded by smaller plaques representing different aspects of Newark's history.

Newark Roundel

The Newark Roundel, a distinctive circular plaque located outside St. Mary Magdalene Church, commemorates the different Newarks of the world

Newark Oriel Windows

Newark is home to a surprising number of oriel windows, a form of bay window that protrudes from the main wall of a building but does not reach the ground. Supported by corbels or brackets, oriel windows are commonly found projecting from upper floors and are a notable feature of the town's architectural heritage.

The Bronze Map of Newark

The bronze map of Newark, located in the Castle Grounds, is a detailed, tactile representation of the town's historical layout. Installed as part of the town's heritage trail, the map highlights significant sites such as Newark Castle, the Church of St. Mary Magdalene, and the Market Square.

Newark Coat of Arms

Granted on December 8, 1561, the Newark Coat of Arms features wavy bars, a crest, and supporters (an otter and a beaver) that refer to Newark's riverside position. The motto, "DEO FRETUS ERUMPE" (Trust God, and sally forth), is a translation of the valiant words of the Mayor during the siege of Newark by the Parliamentarians in 1646.

Newark Cemetery

Established in 1856, Newark Cemetery on London Road features grounds, buildings, and an entrance lodge. The cemetery serves as a place of reflection and remembrance, with sections for the Church of England, Dissenters, and Roman Catholics.

Commonwealth War Graves

Newark Cemetery is home to a significant number of Commonwealth war graves, reflecting the area's historical military importance. The cemetery contains 49 burials from the First World War and a special plot for RAF burials during the Second World War, including 90 Commonwealth burials and 397 Polish burials.

Wilson Street Houses

The terrace of Grade II listed Georgian houses on Wilson Street, built by Dr. Bernard Wilson in 1766, reflects Newark's rich architectural heritage. Wilson, a controversial figure, was a vicar and a wealthy landowner who played a significant role in the town's history.

Newark Town Bowls Club

The Newark Town Bowls Club, established in 1809, is the oldest bowling club in Nottinghamshire. The former clubhouse features a richly ornamented Regency Gothic pediment and an elegant balcony, with an inscription under the balcony reading, "Let no man be biased."

Newark's First Telephone Exchange

Newark's first telephone exchange, built by the National Telephone Company, opened on Portland Street in 1895. The exchange marked the beginning of modern telecommunications in the town.

Alderman Hercules Clay's House

The site of Hercules Clay's House, the Mayor of Newark during the Civil War, is located in the Market Place. Clay had several premonitions of his house being destroyed and moved his family to a safer location just in time.

Ossington Chambers

Ossington Chambers, a terrace of four large houses with steep-pitched roofs, is now used as offices. Built in the 17th-century style, the houses were formerly known as Castle Terrace.

The Arcade
Built in 1897 by the Atter brothers, The Arcade became a fashionable shopping place in Newark. The curved window at the Market Place end was once part of Stanley Noble's small bakery shop known as "Pie Corner".

The Old Mount School
The Old Mount School, with its tower dating from 1877, is a Grade II listed building that has been refurbished as part of a redevelopment project. The schoolroom dates from 1826, and the cross wing to the left of the tower from 1838.

The White House
The White House on Millgate, a substantial mansion dating from the mid-18th century, was once home to Thomas Earp, a maltster, mayor, and Liberal MP for Newark. The house features elaborate Georgian-style internal fittings and a walled garden stretching down to the river.

The Old Railway Line
The Newark to Bottesford railway, open to passenger traffic between 1878 and 1955, offered a route to Nottingham and Leicester. The line is now open to cyclists and pedestrians, providing picturesque views and a peaceful scenic ride between Newark and Cotham.

Notable Historic Sites

Ad Pontem – Newark's Roman Service Station

Long before Newark-on-Trent became known for its castle, Civil War sieges, and excellent tea rooms, it was a strategic pit stop for Roman soldiers, traders, and anyone brave enough to wear sandals year-round. Welcome to Ad Pontem, Latin for "by the bridge" — a name that's as practical as it is poetic.

A Bridge Too Useful

Ad Pontem was established near a crossing of the River Trent, along the Fosse Way, one of Roman Britain's major highways. If you were travelling from Exeter to Lincoln in the 1st century AD (and who wasn't?), this was your go-to layover. Think of it as the Roman equivalent of a motorway service station — only with more spears and fewer overpriced sandwiches.

Fortified Convenience

This wasn't just a roadside snack stop. Ad Pontem featured a fortlet — a small military encampment with ramparts and a double-ditch defensive system. Covering about 1¼ acres, it was designed to keep out troublemakers and keep in the legionnaires. Nearby, a larger polygonal enclosure spanned over 5 acres, with the Fosse Way cutting right through it. Roman efficiency at its finest.

Life at Ad Pontem

The settlement was more than just a military outpost. Archaeological digs have unearthed coins, pottery, glassware, iron tools, and even painted wall plaster — suggesting that some residents lived in style. It was occupied from the late 1st century to at least the 4th century, which means it outlasted most reality TV shows and a few Roman emperors.

Newark's Ancient Neighbour

Though Ad Pontem is technically closer to the village of Brough, its legacy is woven into the fabric of Newark-on-Trent. Artifacts from the site are housed in museums across the region, including Newark itself. So if you're in town and fancy a bit of time travel, pop into the local museum and marvel at the relics of Newark's Roman past.

What's Left Today?

Not much is visible on the surface — unless you're an archaeologist with a drone and a dream. But the site is protected as a Scheduled Monument, and its story continues to intrigue historians and locals alike. It's a reminder that Newark's history didn't start with castles and cannonballs — it started with sandals and stone roads.

Crococalana – The Roman Town That Time (Almost) Forgot

If you've ever driven through the Nottinghamshire countryside and thought, "This field looks suspiciously historic," you might have been passing over the remains of Crococalana—a Roman town with a name that sounds like a prehistoric creature but was, in fact, a thriving settlement just a few miles from modern-day Newark-on-Trent.

What's in a Name?

Crococalana (try saying that three times fast) was a Roman town located near the present-day village of Brough, just northeast of Newark. Its name appears in the Antonine Itinerary, a sort of Roman satnav from the 2nd century AD. While scholars still debate the exact meaning, it's safe to say it was more about roads and rest stops than reptiles.

Location, Location, Legion

Strategically plonked along the Fosse Way, Crococalana was the Roman equivalent of a motorway junction—minus the Greggs. It sat between Margidunum (near Bingham) and Lindum Colonia (modern Lincoln), making it a key stop for soldiers, merchants, and anyone else brave enough to travel in sandals.

The site was a rectangular defended area, roughly 700 by 500 feet, surrounded by ditches. Inside, archaeologists have found crop marks indicating pits, floors, and walls—basically, the Roman version of a housing estate. There's even evidence of a separate enclosure with a rectangular building, possibly a mansio (a kind of Roman Travelodge for officials).

Digging Up the Past

Excavations have unearthed coins, pottery, glassware, iron tools, and objects made of bronze, bone, and horn. The presence of painted wall plaster suggests that some of the buildings were quite posh—think underfloor heating and mosaic envy. Crococalana wasn't just a military outpost; it was a proper town with infrastructure, trade, and probably a few gossiping neighbours.

Newark's Roman Roots

While Crococalana itself lies just outside Newark's modern boundaries, its influence was felt throughout the region. The Fosse Way connected it directly to Ad Pontem and Margidunum, forming a Roman triangle of trade, travel, and tactical advantage. Newark-on-Trent, though not a Roman town itself, owes much of its early development to the infrastructure laid down by these ancient neighbours.

What's There Now?

Today, Crococalana is mostly farmland. No grand ruins, no columns, no toga-clad tour guides. But beneath the soil lies a rich archaeological record, and the site is protected as a Scheduled Monument. Artifacts from Crococalana can be found in museums across the East Midlands, including Newark's own National Civil War Centre—because why not mix your Romans with your Roundheads?

Conclusion: A Town Worth Remembering

Crococalana may not have the fame of Pompeii or the glamour of Rome, but it played a vital role in the Romanisation of Britain—and in the early story of Newark-on-Trent. So next time you're driving past Brough, give a little wave to the fields. You're passing through history, even if it's wearing a very convincing disguise of wheat.

Margidunum – The Roman Roundabout Before Newark

Before Newark-on-Trent became a hotspot for castles, cannonballs, and cream teas, it was surrounded by Roman settlements that made the area a logistical dream for toga-clad travellers. One such place was Margidunum, a name that sounds like a spell from Harry Potter but was actually a bustling Roman town just up the Fosse Way from Newark.

Welcome to the Roman Services

Margidunum, meaning something like "fort by the edge" (or possibly "place where sandals go to die"), was located near modern-day Bingham, just a short chariot ride from Newark. It sat proudly on the Fosse Way, the Roman Empire's answer to the M1, connecting Exeter to Lincoln. If Ad Pontem was the service station with a scenic view, Margidunum was the full-on Roman rest stop—complete with shops, barracks, and probably a few grumpy centurions.

A Fortified Frontier

Established in the 1st century AD, Margidunum began life as a military fort, keeping an eye on the locals and the road. But as the years rolled on and the empire settled in, it evolved into a civilian town. Think less "marching orders" and more "market stalls." Archaeologists have uncovered evidence of roads, buildings, and even a bathhouse—because even Roman soldiers needed a good soak after a long day of empire-building.

What's in a Name?
Margidunum was one of the key waypoints between Ad Pontem and Lindum Colonia (modern-day Lincoln). It was Newark's older, slightly more organised cousin—less drama, more drainage. Its strategic location made it a vital cog in the Roman machine, helping to move troops, goods, and gossip across Britannia.

Digging Up the Past
Excavations at Margidunum have revealed pottery, coins, and the remains of buildings that suggest a community. There's even evidence of a Roman temple, which means the locals weren't just trading—they were praying too. Possibly for better weather or fewer taxes.

Newark's Roman Neighbourhood
While Margidunum itself isn't within Newark's modern boundaries, its influence certainly was. The road that connected it to Ad Pontem ran right through what would become Newark-on-Trent. So, in a way, Newark owes its very existence to the Romans' obsession with straight roads and orderly towns.

Today's Margidunum
Today, there's not much left to see on the surface—unless you're an archaeologist or a very optimistic metal detectorist. But the site is protected, and its story lives on in museums and local lore. If you're ever driving the A46 near Bingham, give a little nod to the fields—you're passing through history.

Queen Sconce

Queen's Sconce in Newark-on-Trent is a significant historical fortification with a rich past. Here's a detailed look at its history

Early History
Queen's Sconce was constructed in 1644 during the First English Civil War to protect the Royalist garrison based at Newark Castle. The fortification was named after Queen Henrietta Maria, the wife of King Charles I. Newark was a key strategic location due to its position at the crossing of the River Trent and the intersection of the Great North Road and Fosse Way.

Architectural Features
The sconce is an earthwork fortification, designed in a star shape when viewed from above1. It measures approximately 120 meters by 133 meters, with a height of up to 9 meters. The structure includes angle bastions projecting from the south, southwest, north, and northeast, which were possible platforms for artillery. The ramparts and bastions are enclosed by a ditch up to 21 meters wide and 4.5 meters deep.

Historical Significance
Queen's Sconce played a crucial role during the sieges of Newark. The town was besieged three times by Parliamentary forces before it finally surrendered in May 1646. The fortification was part of a network of defences that helped the Royalists maintain control over Newark for much of the war. The sconce is one of the few surviving examples of Civil War earthworks in the country

Modern Era

Today, Queen's Sconce is part of Sconce and Devon Park, Newark's largest open space. The park includes a visitor centre, nature reserve, and various recreational facilities. The sconce itself is a listed ancient monument, recognized for its historical and architectural significance. Visitors can explore the fortification and learn about its role in the Civil War through interpretive displays and guided tours.

The Battle of Stoke Field

The Battle of Stoke Field, fought on June 16, 1487, near East Stoke in Nottinghamshire, is considered the last significant battle of the Wars of the Roses. Here's a detailed look at its history

The Wars of the Roses were caused by the protracted struggle for power between the dynasties of the House of Lancaster (red rose) and the competing House of York (white rose).

The battle was the last major conflict between the Houses of York and Lancaster and was a battle to gain control of the crown. The Battle of Bosworth Field, two years previously, had established King Henry VII on the throne, ending the last period of Yorkist rule and initiating that of the Tudors.

Background

The battle was a decisive engagement between the forces of Henry VII, the first Tudor king, and the Yorkist supporters of Lambert Simnel, a pretender to the throne. Despite Henry VII's victory at the Battle of Bosworth in 1485, which ended Richard III's reign and established the Tudor dynasty, Yorkist opposition persisted.

The Battle of Stoke Field was an attempt to unseat King Henry VII in favour of a 10 year old boy called Lambert Simnel who was an imposter pretending to be Edward, Earl of Warwick, the son of Edward IV's brother, the Duke of Clarence. Simnel was used as a pawn by leading Yorkists to try and re-establish their hold on the crown

Key Figures

Henry VII: The reigning king, leading the Lancastrian forces.
John de la Pole, Earl of Lincoln: A leading Yorkist claimant who supported Lambert Simnel.
Lambert Simnel: A young boy presented as Edward, Earl of Warwick, a Yorkist heir.

The Battle

The Yorkist forces, numbering around 8,000, included German and Swiss mercenaries provided by Margaret of Burgundy. They took up a defensive position on Rampire Hill

Henry VII's army, led by the Earl of Oxford, was slightly larger, with about 15,000 men.

The hill they formed up on is known as Burrand Furlong and a stone put there by Newark Archaeological and Local History Society (NALHS) in 1987 marks the spot where Henry VII supposedly planted his standard after the battle. We believe Henry VII's army to have been around 15,000, with John de Vere, Earl of Oxford leading the vanguard of around 6,000 who approached along the Upper Fossse, which crossed what is now Syerston Airfield and continues along Humber Lane and down into the village.

The main battle, led by Henry VII, probably consisted of around 6,000 with the rearguard, led by Lord Strange. It might be worth mentioning the Irish Kerns, who were poorly armed and armoured. One account speaks about them being shot through with arrows 'like hedgehogs' and it was probably there annihilation by the archers that led to the rout. Other key persons involved were Martin Schwartz, leader of the mercenary Landsknechts and Thomas Fitzgerald, leader of the Irish, both of whom were killed.

Outcome

The battle ended in a decisive victory for Henry VII. The Yorkist forces were routed, with many killed in the fighting or pursued and cut down as they fled. Key Yorkist leaders, including the Earl of Lincoln, were killed, effectively ending organized Yorkist resistance.

The Battlefield witnessed the death of up to 7,000 soldiers and the river is said to have ran red with their blood

The Red Gutter is said to be the area where the massacre took place, although it is unclear whether this natural escarpment is so called due the blood split there during the battle or whether it derives its name from red clay deposits.

Historical Significance

The Battle of Stoke Field is often considered the last battle of the Wars of the Roses. It solidified Henry VII's hold on the throne and marked the end of major Yorkist attempts to reclaim it1. The victory also helped to secure the Tudor dynasty's future, allowing Henry VII to focus on consolidating his rule and stabilizing the kingdom

The Newark Torc – Newark's Golden Halo of Mystery

Long before Newark-on-Trent became known for its market stalls, Civil War sieges, and suspiciously enthusiastic reenactors, it was already making headlines — albeit 2,000 years too early for the Newark Advertiser. Enter the Newark Torc: a dazzling Iron Age neck ornament that proves even ancient Britons knew how to accessorise with flair.

Discovery: From Tree Surgeon to Treasure Hunter

In February 2005, Maurice Richardson, a local tree surgeon with a metal detector and a hunch, stumbled upon what would become one of the most significant finds of Iron Age Celtic gold jewellery in half a century. While most of us find bottle caps and rusty nails in fields, Maurice found a 700-gramme gold alloy torc — because Newark doesn't do things by halves

The torc was buried in a pit on the outskirts of town, not lost in a drunken Iron Age stumble as one might hope, but deliberately hoarded. Possibly as an offering to the gods. Or perhaps just hidden by someone who didn't trust Iron Age banks. Either way, it was declared a **national treasure** (just with less Nicholas Cage) and acquired for Newark's Museum (now part of the National Civil War Centre) in 2006, thanks to a hefty grant from the National Heritage Memorial Fund

Design: Gold, Glamour, and a Bit of Norfolk

The Newark Torc is made from a mix of gold, silver, and copper—because plain gold is just too basic. It measures 20 cm in diameter and weighs in at a neck-straining 1.5 pounds. The body is formed from eight finely plaited wires twisted into a single rope, ending in ring-shaped terminals adorned with floral and point-work designs. It's the Iron Age equivalent of haute couture.

Experts believe it was made or finished by the same person as another torc found in Netherurd in Scotland.. This suggests either a travelling goldsmith with a flair for symmetry or a very niche Iron Age Etsy shop.

There is also suggestion that the Torc was stolen by Vikings at one point!!

Purpose: Jewellery, Power Symbol, or Ritual Bling?

What was the torc for? No one knows for sure. It could have been a status symbol, a religious offering, or simply the Iron Age version of a flex. Jeremy Hill of the British Museum described it as "an extraordinary object" showing "an incredibly high level of technological skill and artistry
"
In other words, it wasn't your average neckwear.

Theories abound: perhaps it was worn by a tribal leader, a druid, or someone who just really wanted to be noticed at the local roundhouse gathering. Whatever the case, it was buried with care, suggesting reverence—or at least a very cautious owner.

Legacy: Newark's Shining Star

Today, the Newark Torc is proudly displayed at the National Civil War Centre, where it gleams under glass and sits there, judging your jewellery choices and demanding you add more bling to your life. It's been featured on the BBC, in academic journals, and in the dreams of every amateur detectorist in the East Midlands.

It stands as a testament to Newark's long and glittering history — proof that even in 200 BC, the people of this town had a taste for the finer things. And while we may never know exactly who wore it or why, one thing's certain: Newark-on-Trent has always had a golden touch.

For more info on torcs, check out the fantastic Tess Machlings big book of Torcs - https://bigbookoftorcs.com/

Twelve Sides of Confusion – The Norton Disney Dodecahedron

In the pantheon of archaeological oddities, few objects have inspired as much scholarly head-scratching and speculative mumbling as the Roman dodecahedron. And in 2023, Newark-on-Trent found itself unexpectedly thrust into this ancient enigma when the Norton Disney History and Archaeology Group unearthed one in a field just outside town. Because of course they did.

Discovery: Unearthed by Enthusiasts, Not Aliens

It was June 2023, and while most of the country was busy arguing about potholes and bin days, a group of local archaeologists were digging up history — literally. What they found was a 12-sided copper alloy object, roughly the size of a satsuma, and about as easy to explain. It was the first of its kind discovered in the Midlands and one of only 33 known in Britain. That's rarer than a functioning fax machine.

The object was found in situ (in the original place), nestled beside 4th-century Roman pottery in what appeared to be a quarry pit. It was in excellent condition, which is more than can be said for most of us after a day in the Nottinghamshire sun.

Description: A Dodecahedron by Any Other Name

The Norton Disney Dodecahedron is made of 75% copper, 7% tin, and 18% lead—basically the Roman version of a mystery meat pie. Each of its twelve pentagonal faces has a circular hole in the centre, and the whole thing is cast with a level of precision that suggests either ritual significance or a very bored metallurgist.

It's not standardised in size, shows no signs of wear, and doesn't appear in any Roman texts. Which means it's either a sacred object, a child's toy, or the ancient equivalent of a paperweight that no one wanted to admit they didn't understand.

Theories: Ritual, Religion, or Really No Idea

Scholars have proposed everything from candlestick holders to astronomical devices to knitting gauges. But the most plausible theory is that these dodecahedra were used in religious or ritual contexts—possibly linked to the mounted horseman deity discovered nearby in 1989. Because nothing says "divine power" like a twelve-holed polygon.

Of course, it could also have been a very elaborate way to lose your marbles.

Legacy: Newark's Most Mathematical Mystery

Today, the Norton Disney Dodecahedron is proudly displayed at the National Civil War Centre in Newark, where it silently judges visitors who can't remember their GCSE geometry (te smug little scamper). It's also been featured on the BBC's *Digging for Britain*, which is the archaeological equivalent of being knighted.

The Myth of the Newark Tunnels

Newark-on-Trent is a town rich in history, with tales of kings, battles, and ancient architecture. But among its many stories, one persistent myth has captured the imagination of locals and visitors alike: the legend of the Newark Tunnels.

A Town Beneath the Town?

For generations, rumors have swirled about a network of tunnels running beneath Newark. These subterranean passages are said to connect various historic sites, from the castle to the church, and even to the Friary. The idea of secret tunnels used for clandestine activities, hidden escapes, or smuggling has a certain romantic allure. But is there any truth to these tales?

The Wing Tavern and Other Legends

One of the most famous tunnel tales involves the Wing Tavern pub, which reportedly had a door in the cellar floor leading to a mysterious passage. However, personal accounts suggest that this "tunnel" was merely a short length of cellar heading towards the church. Similarly, rumors of a tunnel between the Friary, Newark Castle, and the church have never been substantiated.

The Search for Evidence

Over the years, various investigations have sought to uncover the truth behind the tunnel myth. In 2013, an archaeological study using ground-penetrating radar found no evidence of tunnels under the Market Place, though it did reveal extended cellars and medieval walls.
A 2014 documentary explored the cellars beneath shops around the town, but failed to establish any concrete connections.

In 2018, a more extensive radar survey funded by lottery money aimed to settle the question once and for all. The results were disappointing for tunnel enthusiasts: no tunnels were found, only extensive cellars. Kevin Winter of the Newark Town Centre Hidden Heritage Group noted that while the findings were not definitive, they strongly suggested that the tunnels were a myth.

Why the Myth Persists

Despite the lack of evidence, the tunnel myth endures. Perhaps it's the allure of hidden history, or the thrill of imagining secret passages beneath our feet. Or maybe it's just the fun of a good story. As James Wright, a building archaeologist, points out, tales of underground passages are common in many towns and villages. They often connect contrasting locations, like a manor house and a nunnery, adding a hint of scandal to the mix.

The Practicalities of Tunnel Building

The geology of Newark makes the construction of extensive tunnels unlikely. Unlike Nottingham, which is riddled with tunnels due to its sandstone base, Newark's clay-based soil and proximity to the river would have made tunnel construction difficult. The tunnels would have been hard to keep secret, expensive to build, and challenging to maintain.

The Final Verdict

While the idea of tunnels beneath Newark is tantalizing, the evidence suggests that they are more myth than reality. The interconnected cellars, extended for practical purposes like storage during the coaching era, likely gave rise to the tunnel tales. As Mr. Winter aptly put it, "People have loved to believe there were tunnels under Newark."

So, the next time you hear a story about the Newark Tunnels, enjoy it for what it is: a charming piece of local folklore that adds a touch of mystery to this historic town.

Fun Fact

The Wing Tavern pub was opened in protest by a landlord who was forced to close the Green Dragon pub to allow the final wing of the town hall to be built. The last remaining part of this pub is now known as Newark's thinnest house.

The Old Walls and Gates of Newark-on-Trent

Newark-on-Trent once boasted impressive walls and gates that encircled its medieval heart. While no physical remains of these ancient fortifications exist today, their legacy lives on through historical records, archaeological findings, and local lore.

The Elusive Walls

The old walls of Newark are a bit of a mystery. None of the existing plans show them, and the oldest maps only depict the town's defenses during the sieges, which were outside the line of the main walls. However, we can piece together their estimated locations based on historical accounts and the positions of the town's gates.

Mapping the Walls

Using various accounts, we can estimate the location of the walls. The walls possibly started at Trent Bridge, following the present line of Brewery Lane, Slaughterhouse Lane, and the Mount to Appleton Gate. From there, the wall turned south, running across Chauntry Park, behind the old Grammar School, and slightly east of Barnby Gate House. It then crossed Balderton Gate, turned southwest to Carter Gate, and continued down the north side of what is now Lombard Street (formerly Potterdyke) before crossing Castle Gate and reaching the river.

The Gates of Newark

Newark had three main gates: North Gate, East Gate, and South Gate. These gates were crucial for controlling access to the town and were often the focal points of defense during times of conflict.

North Gate (North Bar Gate)

Located near the current corner of Northgate and Slaughterhouse Lane, the North Gate was a stone wall with an arch, demolished in 1762. It was described as having a tall, narrow arch formed of thin slabs, with a double course of radially set voussoirs. This gate was a key entry point to the town from the north.

East Gate (Dry Bridge)

The East Gate, also known as Dry Bridge, stood in the middle of Bridge Street, near where Birds Bakery is today. It was taken down in 1784. Dr. Stukeley described it as a fine old arched gate of Roman work, with arches that were discovered during rebuilding efforts. The gate's position is now represented by buildings on either side of Bridge Street.

South Gate

The South Gate's position is defined in local deeds, indicating it was located at the end of Milnegate, near the corner of Pottergate. This gate controlled access to the town from the south and was an important part of Newark's defenses.

Archaeological Findings

Despite the lack of visible remains, archaeological studies have provided some insights into Newark's old walls. In 2013, a ground-penetrating radar survey found no evidence of tunnels under the Market Place but did locate extended cellars and earlier walls, likely dating back to medieval times. Further surveys in 2018 supported the idea that the town's defenses were primarily earthen ramparts rather than stone walls.

This is just a glimpse into Newark's architectural heritage. **www.newarkguide.co.uk** includes everything from former maltings and breweries to telephone kiosks and war memorials.

More Books by David Fargher

For All Ages

Available via www.newarkguide.co.uk/shop

Colette and the Watch of Time: Newark"

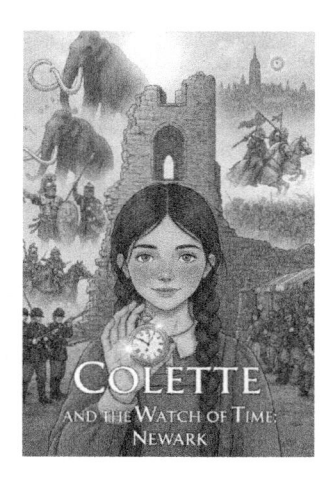

Join Colette, a girl with a magical pocket watch, as she tumbles through time to explore the amazing history of Newark-on-Trent! From dodging woolly mammoths in the Ice Age to building ancient henges, and from bustling Roman roads to the dramatic English Civil War, Colette experiences it all firsthand.

This isn't just history; it's a hilarious, whirlwind adventure through 14,000 years, bringing Newark's incredible past to life with every turn of her watch. Get ready for a fun-filled journey that proves history is anything but boring!

Perfect for curious kids (ages 7-12) who love adventure and magic, and for parents and educators looking for a fun way to bring history to life. It's also a charming read for anyone with a connection to Newark-on-Trent, eager to see their town's unique story unfold.

Newark On Trent Colouring Book

The Town By The River
Created By www.newarkguide.co.uk

Discover Newark-on-Trent like never before with this fun and educational colouring book!

Perfect for kids and curious minds of all ages, this beautifully designed book features **10 detailed illustrations of Newark's most iconic historic sites with descriptions** — ready for you to bring to life with colour,.

This book also features a **timeline** and **story of Newarks history.**

Whether you're a local or a visitor, this colouring book is a creative way to explore the heritage of Newark-on-Trent and learn while having fun!

A Special Creative Treat

Have fun!
:)

All pictures converted from Photos taken by Dave Fargher

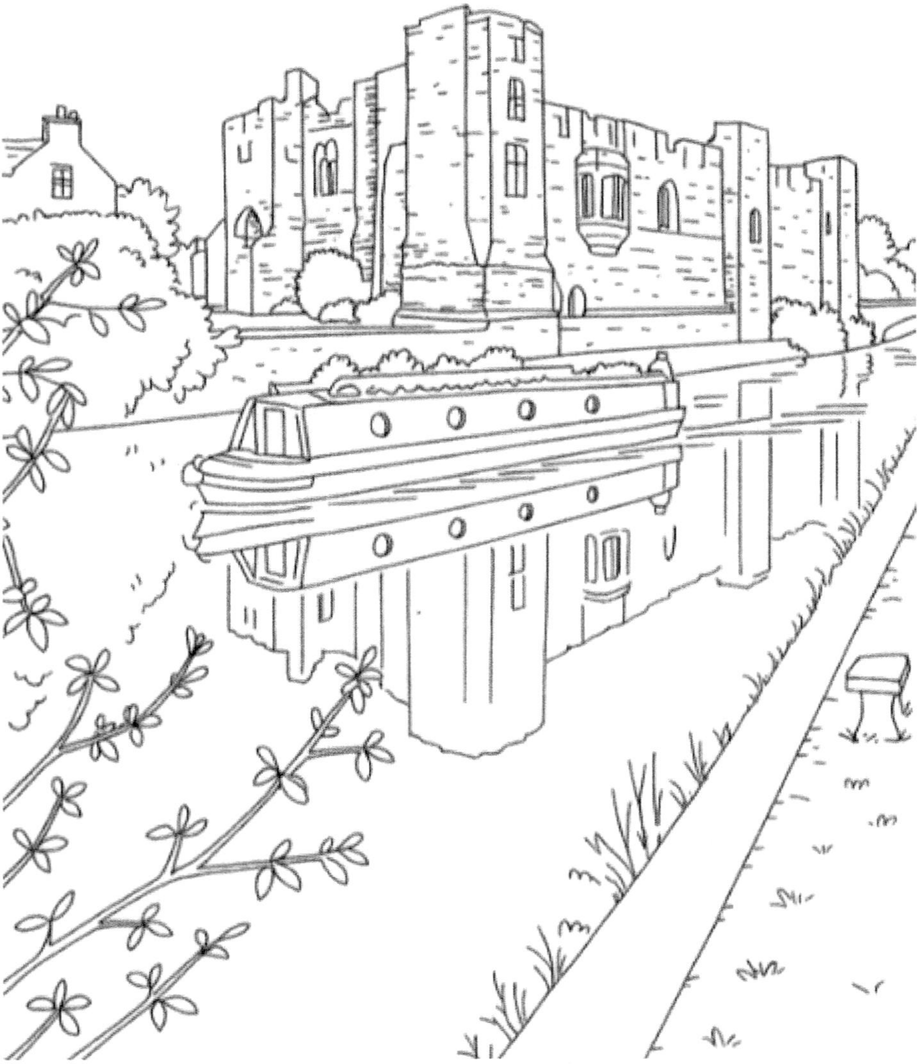

149

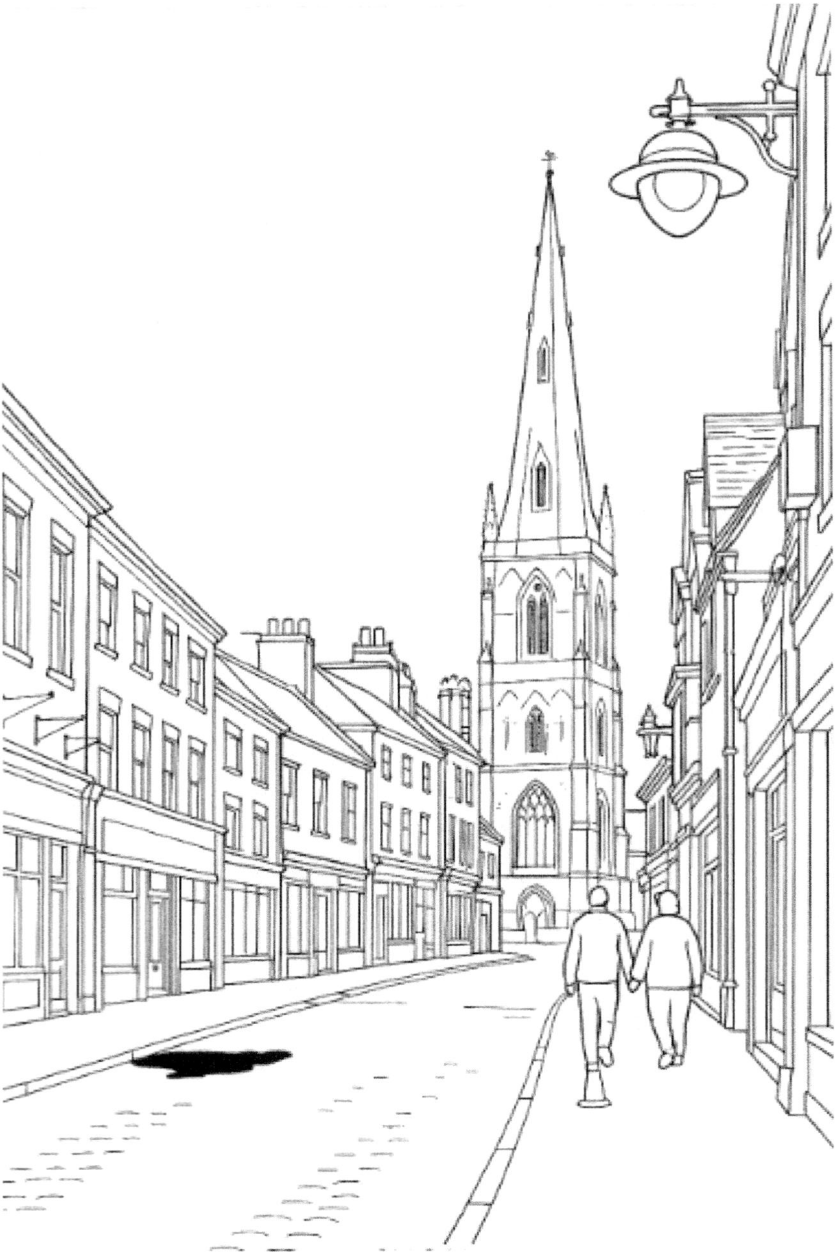

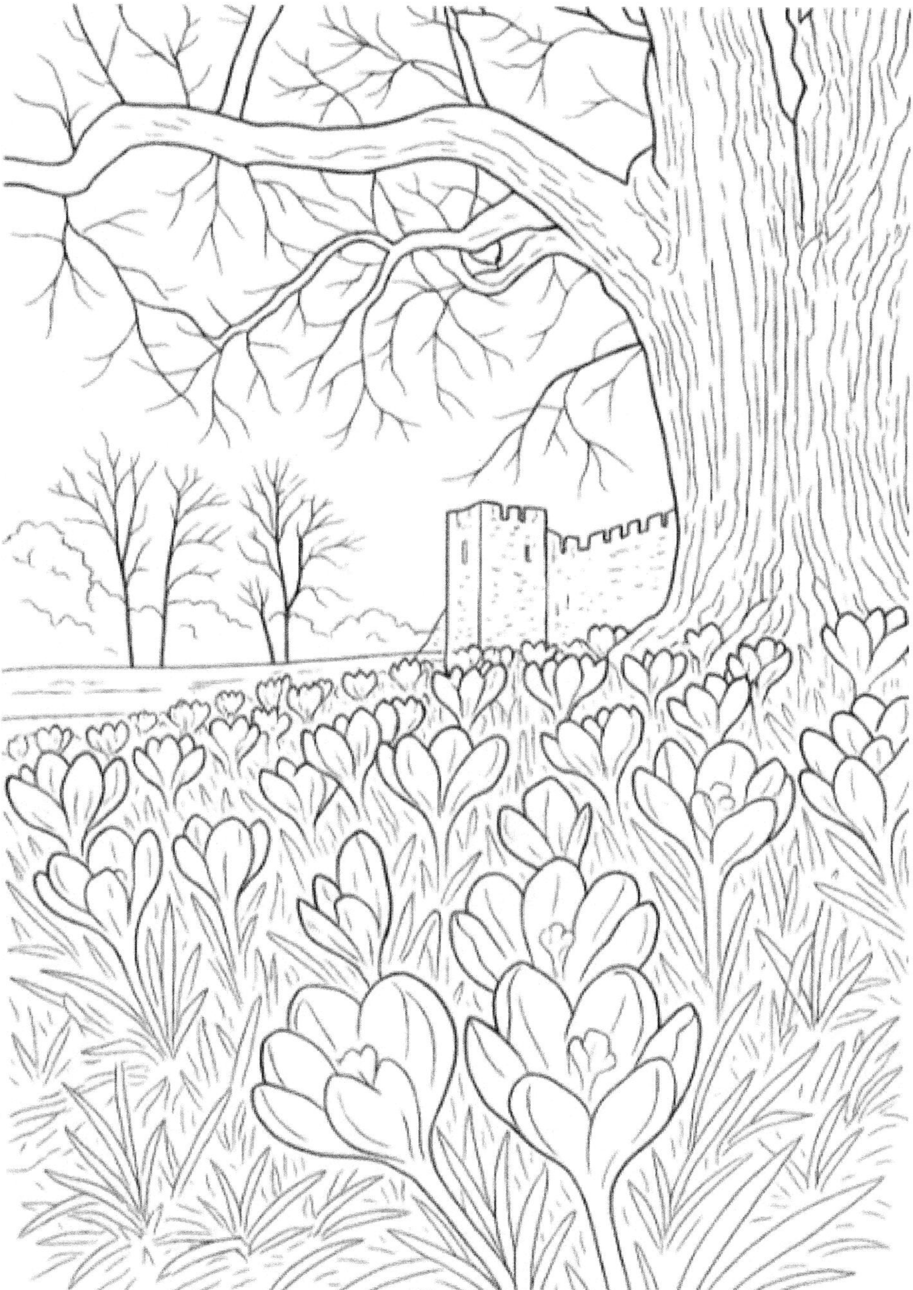

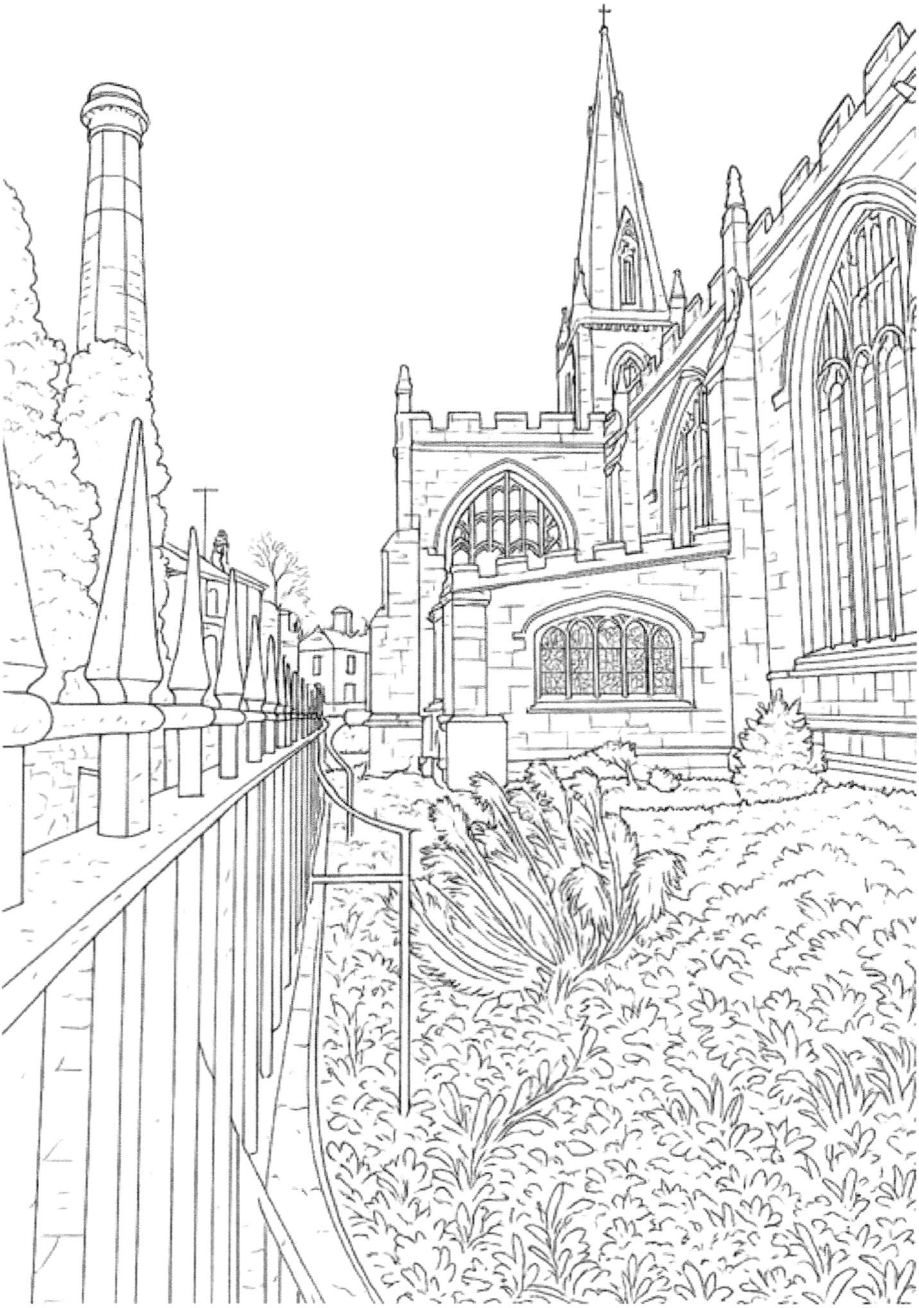

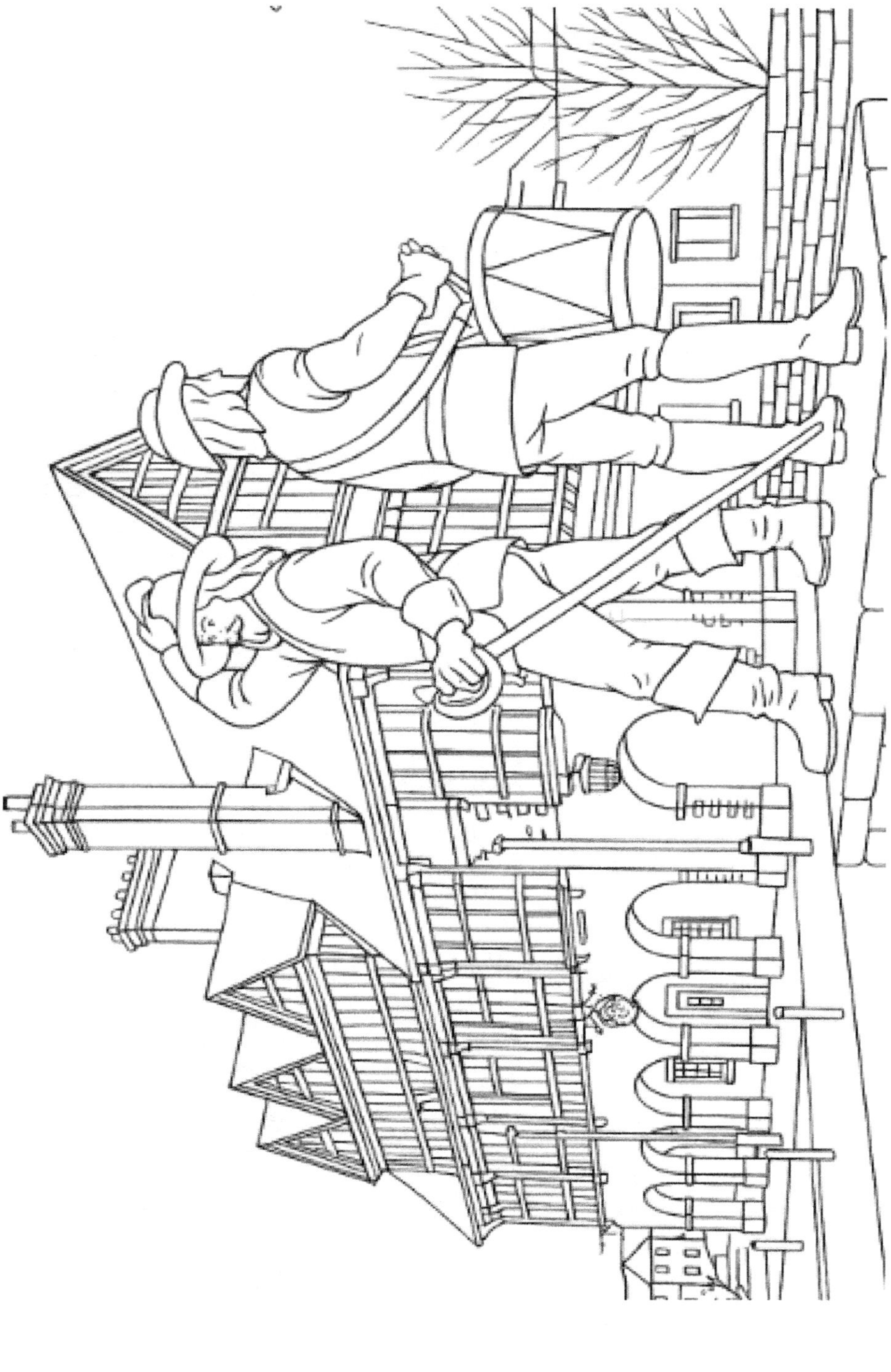

154

Designed and Created by Dave Fargher

Thanks.

WWW.NEWARKGUIDE.CO.UK

IMMERSE YOURSELF IN THE CAPTIVATING HISTORY OF NEWARK-ON-TRENT, NOTTINGHAMSHIRE.

WE ARE DEDICATED TO SHOWCASING THE LOCAL HISTORIC SITES, SHARING STORIES OF THE RESIDENTS, AND PRESERVING THE ESSENCE OF OUR TOWN'S PAST FOR GENERATIONS TO COME.

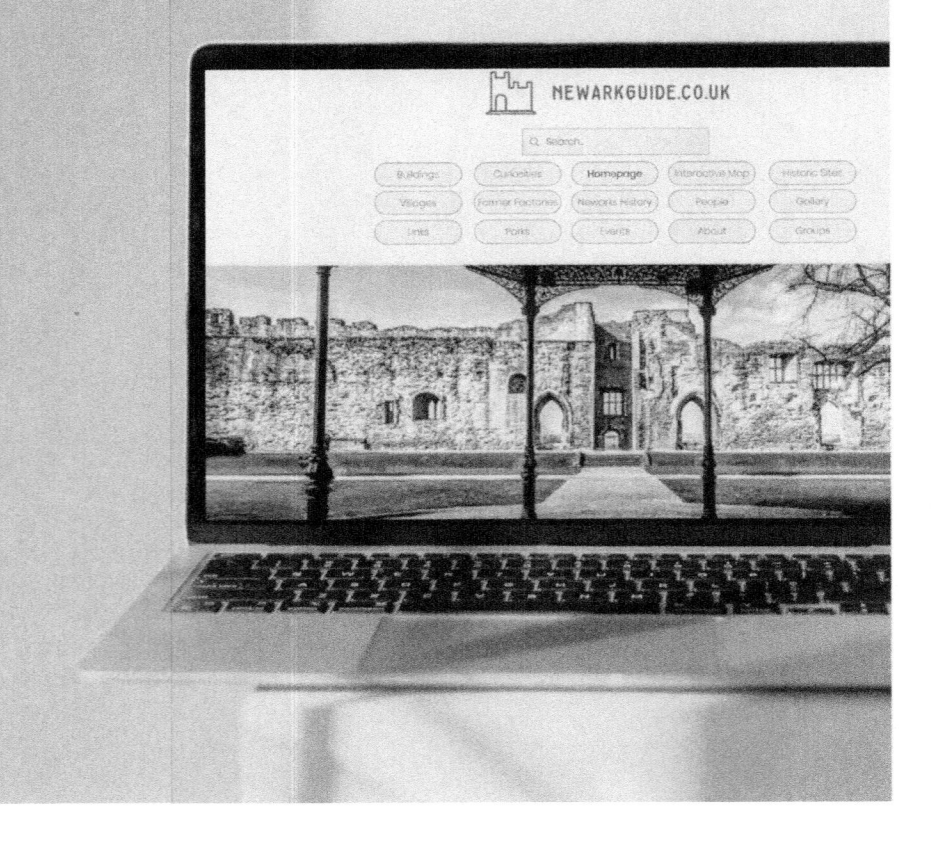

Free Guide to Newark on Trent

For anyone new or existing visiting the town, Newark Guide contains a wealth of information on Newark's fascinating history, from its pre-historic roots to its industrial heyday, Curiosities and sites, Events, groups and the people who have shaped the town and continue to do so.

Newark Guide – www.newarkguide.co.uk

Visitors can explore a treasure trove of information, including:

Historic Sites and buildings:
Discover the town's iconic landmarks, such as the imposing Newark Castle, and delve into their captivating histories, including once-thriving industries, factories, warehouses and the impact they had on its development.

Curiosities:
Find out more about lesser known sites and places that you may never know existed

A full history of Newark going back 14,000 years
The Myth of The Newark Tunnels
The Old town Walls
Town Trails

Interactive maps:
Navigate the town and surrounding areas with a free interactive maps.

Search function:
Simply search any key word to bring up related information

Local Legends:
Uncover fascinating tales of the people who have shaped

Newark's past, from renowned figures to artists, famous faces to everyday heroes.

Surrounding Villages:
Explore the charming villages that surround Newark, each with its own distinct history and character.

Also included:
Photo & Video gallery

Parks and public spaces
Useful links & Contact
Events around the town
Commmunity Groups
Useful Info about visiting

If you enjoy taking photos, please do share any of our beautiful town to Newark-on-Trent Photographs